To Dana

Anne Korin and Gal Luft

PETROPOLY

The Collapse of America's Energy Security Paradigm

The first and most urgent necessity in the area of government policy is the elimination of those measures which directly support monopoly.

Milton Friedman

CONTENTS

LIST OF ACRONYMS

AMFA   Alternative Motor Fuels Act
CAFE   Corporate Average Fuel Economy
CARB   California Air Resources Board
CBO   Congressional Budget Office
CCS   Carbon Capture and Sequestration
CNG   Compressed Natural Gas
CNOOC   China National Offshore Oil Corporation
CO   Carbon monoxide
DOE   Department of Energy
EIA   Energy Information Administration
EISA   Energy Independence and Security Act of 2007
EPA   Environmental Protection Agency
Eroei   Energy return on energy invested
EV   Electric Vehicle
FFV   Flexible Fuel Vehicle
GE   Gasoline Ethanol
GEM   Gasoline Ethanol Methanol
gge   Gasoline gallon equivalent
GHG   Greenhouse Gas
GMA   Grocery Manufacturers Association
GTL   Gas to Liquids
HOV   High Occupancy Vehicle
IEA   International Energy Agency
IOC   International Oil Companies
LNG   Liquefied Natural Gas
LPG   Liquefied Petroleum Gas
b/d   barrels per day
mmbtu   Million British Thermal Units
MTBE   Methyl tertiary butyl ether
NDRC   National Development and Reform Commission
NERC   North American Electric Reliability Corporation
NOC   National Oil Companies
NOPEC   No Oil Producing and Exporting Cartels Act
NOx   Nitrogen oxide
OFID   Fund for International Development
OFS   Open Fuel Standard
OPEC   Organization of Petroleum Exporting Countries
PDVSA   Petróleos de Venezuela, S.A
PHEV   Plug-in Hybrid Electric Vehicle
RFS   Renewable Fuel Standard
SAMA   Saudi Arabian Monetary Agency
TRC   Texas Railroad Commission
VEETC   Volumetric Ethanol Excise Tax Credit
VMT   Vehicle Miles Traveled
WTI   West Texas Intermediate
WTO   World Trade Organization

A NOTE ON TERMINOLOGY

Gas shale is a sedimentary rock containing trapped natural gas molecules. The gas extracted from the rock using hydraulic fracturing and horizontal drilling technologies is called *shale gas*.

Oil shale is a sedimentary rock containing hydrocarbon rich kerogen. The oil found and extracted from the shale is called *shale oil*. Shale oil should not be confused with *tight oil*. Tight oil is light crude oil contained in petroleum-bearing formations of relatively low porosity and permeability such as in North Dakota, Texas and other shale formations. Tight oil is extracted in a method similar to the extraction of shale gas - fracking and horizontal drilling. Shale oil, on the other hand, is extracted by mining and crushing the rock and then heating it above ground to a temperature of 570°F, beyond which the kerogen begins to decompose into usable hydrocarbon. Alternatively, the rock can be heated underground through the insertion of very high temperature (above 900°F) heaters deep into the ground. While tight oil is extractable economically, both methods of shale oil extraction are not yet competitive with conventional crude.

Oil sands, or tar sands, are sticky, black, tar-like mixtures of sand, clay and water saturated with a dense and viscous form of petroleum referred to as bitumen. This type of heavy crude oil is so thick that it must be heated or diluted before it will flow in pipelines.

Unconventional oil and gas are produced or extracted using techniques other than the conventional well method. One should not confuse between *unconventional oil* and *heavy oil*. Some unconventional oils, like tar sands, are heavy while others, like tight oil, are light.

PROLOGUE

Once upon a time, there was a shining city upon a hill. It was a fine city. "A tall proud city built on rocks stronger than oceans, wind-swept, God-blessed, and teeming with people of all kinds living in harmony and peace, a city with free ports that hummed with commerce and creativity, and if there had to be city walls, the walls had doors and the doors were open to anyone with the will and the heart to get there," in the words of one of its leaders.[1] But there was one problem. A big problem. The people of the city suffered from a rare affliction, a genetic disorder which prevented them from digesting any food protein other than salmon. No beef, no chicken, no eggs, no tuna, not even soy. Only salmon. Smoked, baked, grilled or raw, the city's dwellers found many ways to prepare their salmon. Gourmet chefs prepared the delicate fish to suit every possible palate. Burger joints served salmon patties, pizza parlors sprinkled salmon cubes on their dough, and salmon rolls were the pride of the city's sushi restaurants. Salmon casserole was the yummiest of all, and tourists from throughout the world flocked to the city to taste this delicacy.

Overall, life was good. But there was always great anxiety about the future. What would happen if the salmon supply were interrupted? This concern was not unfounded. The city's river was overfished, and the salmon population was dwindling as the city's population was growing. As the years went by, the city became increasingly dependent on imported salmon which was supplied primarily by the city's not-so-friendly northern neighbors - a dysfunctional bunch. Every few years when the northern neighbors fought each other, their salmon exports tanked and prices soared. One day, when they were not busy fighting each other, in a rare moment of unity, the salmon exporters colluded to form OSEC, the Organization of Salmon Exporting Countries. They met every few months to discuss how much salmon to farm and what price to charge their clients. Since they too had growing salmon-loving populations they were forced to divert much of their production to the local market leaving less fish to export. As salmon prices skyrocketed, the city was forced to spend more and more of its money on imports and the population went deeper into debt to finance its diet.

No longer willing to stand for OSEC's shenanigans, the city's people decided to take action to reduce their vulnerability. At first, they invested much of their budget in forming a formidable military. With such might, the northern neighbors would not dare use their salmon exports as a tool of coercion, it was thought. In an attempt to reach "salmon independence," aqua-farming became a high priority for the city. The rationale was: if we only learned how to farm fish, we could become self-sufficient in food. But as portrayed in the film *Fishing for Salmon in the Yemen,* salmon farming was not an easy endeavor. Every few years, mysterious diseases hit the farm-raised salmon population and the city's medical research centers spent almost as much of their resources on fish medicine as on human health.

One day, concerned citizens started a new movement with a bold idea: instead of spending ever growing amounts of money on securing access to harder and harder to obtain salmon, let's invest our resources on advancing gene therapy solutions aimed at diversifying the city's diet. "If we could only find and alter the gene that restricts our diet, the door will forever be open for us and our descendants to consume every other form of protein whether from animal or plant," they stated. This made a lot of sense. Sure enough, it would be a formidable undertaking but so was the maintenance of the large army, the periodic salmon wars, the servicing of the ballooning national debt and the ever growing healthcare costs associated with poor diet. Unlocking our bellies to food competition would be, as one pundit put it, "a win-win-win-win situation."

But there were naysayers galore. Among the skeptics were various politically powerful defenders of the status quo like the Domestic Fishermen's Alliance, the Association of Bait Manufacturers, the Salmon Institute and the Fishing Boats Mechanics Union. All of them had huge sway over local politicians, and all of them were committed to put their resources to work and kill "Project Independence." The idea of competition with salmon was particularly terrifying to OSEC. For decades, members of the cartel bet their future on income derived from salmon exports. A cure to salmon dependency would be a crippling blow to their economies. This gene therapy nonsense had to be stopped.

Scientists were recruited, studies were commissioned, PR firms were hired, and conferences were held all with one objective in mind: Convince voters that food flexibility is a recklessly radical idea, with the potential unintended consequences of genetic engineering. "Why rock the fishing boat and introduce new food? Salmon is the most nutritious food and for centuries our diet served us well. Beef and tofu will only make us sicker," argued the detractors. "Salmon is the bedrock of our culture. Moving from salmon to food competition is like adopting paganism";

"Keep newfangled food off of our plates;" "Why throw good money on junk science when our enemies are gaining strength and our military is falling behind?" Experts were summoned to lecture about the looming risks of Mad Cow Disease, Avian Flu, Salmonella and other health hazards afflicting the rest of humanity.

The detractors' campaign of disinformation and fear mongering worked. It was the end of a dream and the beginning of a nightmare. Years of hunger, wars, and economic decline followed. The northern neighbors gained incredible amounts of wealth, hollowing out the city's economy. Poor protein intake hindered brain development among the city's children, and the education level fell. Stagnant and decaying, the city upon a hill was going downhill. What once used to be a city of hope became a city of despair.[1]

Could this city be us?

INTRODUCTION:
BARKING UP THE WRONG TREE

Though this be madness, yet there is method in it.
Polonius in William Shakespeare's Hamlet

More than a decade has passed since the vicious attacks of a terrible September morning. Our memory of that day is vivid, and the link between oil's status as a strategic commodity and the protected status of the countries most responsible for proliferating the hatred that fueled those attacks is visceral. It has been the driving force of our work over the past decade. Perhaps you feel the same way. We are not going to delve into the national security implications of oil in this book, because nothing we say will convince you if you haven't made the connection already. And in any case if you want to read more about that, you'll find our arguments in the book's prequel titled *Turning Oil into Salt: Energy Independence through Fuel Choice.*[1]

The past several years have also brought an entirely unsurprising economic downturn. We'd never argue that the oil price spike of 2008 was the sole or even primary reason for the economic doldrums this country has been suffering through, but it was certainly the gusting wind that tipped over a tower built on shoddy foundations of unsustainable government spending, unsecured private debt, and a great deal of wishful – perhaps even utopian – thinking. And the budget busting highs in oil prices since 2006 have, along with a variety of other factors, served as stumbling blocks to economic recovery.

Over the past decade working on the oil issue we've realized that the tendency of many of those thinking about energy security, including nearly every president going back to Dwight D. Eisenhower, has been to gravitate to the concrete and measurable rather than the abstract. That's unsurprising, and in some areas of problem solving actually quite useful – after all, if you cannot measure outcomes, how do you characterize success? But when it comes to oil, the tendency to gravitate toward the measurable has led policy makers and pundits to focus on the wrong problem by equating oil dependence to America's level of oil imports, to proffer solutions intent on addressing that incorrectly defined problem, and to assume that the vulnerabilities – economic, security – associated with oil dependence will be alleviated should that wrongly defined problem be addressed and oil imports into the United States decrease. We wrote this book to bring that misdefinition into sharp relief, and to – hopefully – recalibrate national thinking on oil to a more accurate problem definition and thus to solutions that have a chance of getting America – not to mention the rest of the world – out of the mire.

A misguided fixation

As Supreme Allied Commander in World War II, Dwight D. Eisenhower witnessed the impact oil dependency had on the German and Japanese war machines and how those countries' strategic choices were shaped by their desperate need for petroleum. As president, he was convinced that the growing level of oil imports posed a challenge to America's world hegemony. To avoid this vulnerability, his administration imposed mandatory import quotas favoring Western Hemispheric oil exporters to those from the Middle East, capping foreign oil imports at 12 percent of domestic production.[2]

The emergence of the Organization of Petroleum Exporting Countries (OPEC) in the 1960's, the 1973-74 Arab Oil Embargo, the 1978 Iranian Revolution and the Iran-Iraq War all aggravated America's sense of vulnerability. Every President since Richard Nixon adopted oil import reduction as the core of his energy policy. On January 30, 1974, with 34 percent of America's net oil needs coming from foreign sources, President Nixon said in his State of the Union Address: "Let this be our national goal: at the end of this decade, in the year 1980, the United States will not be dependent on any other country for the energy we need to provide our jobs, to heat our homes, and to keep our transportation moving."[3] The following year, President Gerald Ford pledged: "We must reduce oil imports by one million barrels per day by the end of this year and by two million barrels per day by the end of 1977."[4] One year later he announced: "I signed a compromise national energy bill which enacts a part of my comprehensive energy independence program [...] to make America invulnerable to the foreign oil cartel."[5]

Shortly after, the Iranian Revolution erupted, and the Persian Gulf was set on fire with a bloody war between Iran and Iraq. Oil prices soared, and America, with 37 percent of its oil needs from foreign sources, was again in a recession. On July 15, 1979 President Jimmy Carter delivered his famous Crisis of Confidence Speech pledging: "Beginning this moment, this nation will never use more foreign oil than we did in 1977 – never."[6] Two years later, he was back on his Georgia peanut farm and it was President Ronald Reagan's turn to assert that "The best answer [. . .] is to try to make us independent of outside sources to the greatest extent possible for our energy."[7] Another eight years came and went, oil prices collapsed and United States foreign oil dependence dropped for a few years only to bounce back to a 40 percent level during the presidency of George H.W. Bush, who in his 1989 State of the Union Address, promised: "the gulfs and oceans off our shores hold the promise of oil and gas reserves which can make our nation more secure and less dependent on foreign oil."[8] That worked so well that five years later United States oil import dependence grew to 45 percent, and President Bill Clinton warned: "The nation's growing reliance on imports of oil threatens the nation's security." His solution: "[we] will continue efforts to [. . .] enhance domestic energy production."[9] Clinton left office soon after, but imports were going nowhere but up. President George W. Bush, who despite his strong ties to the oil industry stated that "America is addicted to oil," governed during a period of massive turmoil in global oil markets: war in the Middle East, concerns about terrorism against oil infrastructure, the rise of China and at the same time relative prosperity in the developed world which drove up the demand for crude. For the first time since the 1970s, the problem of oil dependence moved back to the center of the public's attention. Bush's first State of the Union Address after September 11 highlighted the oil vulnerability. He called on Congress to "increase energy production at home so America is less dependent on foreign oil," and in his second term, in 2006 with U.S. oil import dependence reaching its highest level ever, 60 percent, he declared "a great goal": "to replace more than 75 percent of our oil imports from the Middle East by 2025."[10] With dreams of self-sufficiency deeply engraved in America's political DNA, President Barack Obama was not about to break the mold. "It will be the policy of my administration to reverse our dependence on foreign oil while building a new energy economy that will create millions of jobs," he pledged in 2009 and repeatedly thereafter.[11]

These nine presidents differed only in the remedies they offered to the "import problem": Republicans emphasized supply side solutions − "Drill-Baby-Drill"; Democrats called for an oil diet, using less oil through taxation or increased fuel economy standards. But while their solutions varied, they have all shared the conviction that America's energy security vulnerability would be alleviated if only the country imported less oil. The rationale for this was best described by Professor Michael Mandelbaum, one of America's most respected foreign policy experts. In his 2010 book, *The Frugal Superpower: America's*

Global Leadership in a Cash-Strapped Era, Mandelbaum made a strong case for making the Middle East "less important." He observed that "the Middle East matters because the world depends heavily on its oil. Since the United States uses so much oil, a major reduction in American consumption would substantially lower the global total. [...] The less oil the world uses, the less important the region that has so much of it becomes," he opined. So far so good. But here goes Mandelbaum to commit a most common mistake:

> The best way to reduce oil use is to raise the price of gasoline. People would then use less of it. In the short term, they would drive less and make more use of public transportation. Over the long term, they would demand fuel-efficient vehicles. [...] The refusal of the U.S. to charge itself as much for gasoline as is good for it (and for other countries) is the single greatest foreign policy failure of the past three decades. Correcting that failure will not be easy. [...] Such an effort, however, would be worthwhile. Reducing oil consumption by raising the gasoline tax would once again make the U.S. a resolute and effective global leader. Unlike the Administration's diplomatic initiatives, it would not require the cooperation of the governments or people of other countries. Most important of all, as a strategy for shielding Americans from the dangers of the Middle East, it would certainly succeed.[12]

Regretfully, as we will show, this is not the case. President after president, along with thousands of members of Congress, academics and pundits like Mandelbaum who have shaped the energy policy discourse in recent decades failed to correctly diagnose the root of America's oil vulnerability. When a problem is not diagnosed correctly, one needs tremendous luck for the remedies to address the real issue. America has not been so lucky.

The energy security paradox

Over the past decade, America's energy landscape has seemed to change significantly. According to the Department of Energy, United States net imports of petroleum declined from 12.5 million barrels per day (b/d) in 2005 to 7.7 million b/d in 2012.[13] Our import dependency dropped from its 60 percent peak to 42 percent, the level it was in 1990. This 38 percent reduction in the level of imports, equivalent to three times the number of barrels imported from Saudi Arabia in just seven years, is a non-trivial achievement. Some of this is, of course, due to the recession: as the price of fuel rises, people find ways to lower their discretionary driving. But for the most part the reduction has to do with a dramatic ramp up in domestic oil production, increased ethanol blending, and improvement in vehicle fuel efficiency - new cars and trucks sold today are 20 percent more efficient than in 2007.[14] Since 2008, America's innovative oil industry, deploying ever evolving technologies like deepwater drilling, hydraulic fracturing and horizontal drilling, has increased crude oil output by over 20 percent. In 2011 alone, onshore rig count in the United States grew by 30 percent. About a million barrels per day emerged from a new source, "tight oil," which is extracted with hydraulic fracturing technology from petroleum bearing geological formations. North Dakota – the center of the tight-oil transformation – has emerged from a virtual nobody in America's oil landscape to the fourth largest oil-producing state, behind Texas, Alaska and California. For the first time in decades, the United States is experiencing an oil boom, or at least a boomlet. Forecasts show that oil imports may be past their 2005 peak, and are likely to remain roughly flat over the next 20 years.[15] A Harvard University study predicts that by 2020 the United States could be the world's second largest oil producer after Saudi Arabia.[16] Goldman Sachs went even further, predicting that it will become the largest oil-producing country by 2017.[17]

But here is the rub. Simple economics suggest that *in a competitive market* if demand falls and supply rises, prices should fall. The exact opposite has happened. While America's oil imports dropped, oil price went up, and foreign oil expenditures climbed by almost 50 percent, from $247 billion in 2005 to $367 billion in 2011. The share of oil imports in the overall trade deficit grew from 32 percent in 2005 to 58 percent in 2011. Worse: the price of a gallon of regular gasoline in 2005 was $2.30. By the spring of 2012 the national average of regular gasoline surpassed $4. In 2011, American drivers spent more money on gasoline than in any other year before. Against the expectations of many energy self-sufficiency advocates, the volume of America's imports and the cost of its imports moved in opposite directions. In the past decade we seemingly did the right things: we both drilled and improved the fuel efficiency of our cars. As a result we became more self-sufficient. So how come we became poorer and deeper in debt? How come our gasoline expenditures are higher than ever? If one accepts the traditional definition of energy security as "availability of sufficient supply at affordable prices," then we have gained some points on the availability front only to lose many more on the affordability side of the ledger. And at a time of economic adversity, it is the latter that matters more. Could it be that something is wrong with our method?

Our leaders have all focused on our dependence on oil imports, when the real problem is not the number of oil barrels we import or even the number of barrels we use – we don't care how many bananas we consume or how much coffee we import. The problem is not even our dependence on Persian Gulf oil. Contrary to popular thinking, only ten percent – yes, ten percent – of our oil supply originates in the Persian Gulf. In fact, at no point in history did the region provide more than 15 percent of our oil. The real problem is that first, while oil demand has fallen and supply has grown in the U.S., globally neither is the case, and second, we are not in a competitive market.

The oil market is dominated by the OPEC cartel, which sits on 78 percent of the world's conventional oil reserves. Yet, this group has restricted production capacity to the point that it accounts for just over a third of oil supply, and it has a chokehold on the global economy because oil has a virtual monopoly over transportation fuel.

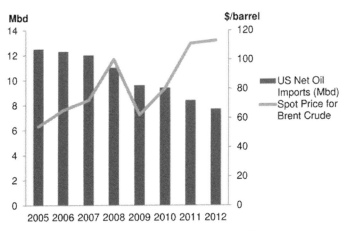

The energy security paradox: we import less but pay more

Turn oil into salt

As we pointed out in *Turning Oil into Salt*, oil today enjoys the status salt used to enjoy for many centuries.[18] Because it was the sole means of food preservation, human beings depended on ample supply of affordable salt for their survival. Those who had no salt could not preserve enough meat, fish and vegetables during the summer to survive the harsh winter months. Wars were fought over salt; colonies were built around it and in the 17th century British leaders spoke with urgency about the dangerous national dependence on French salt. All this changed in the year 1800 in

Napoleonic France. Malnutrition was a major problem for the 18th century French Army and a major operational problem for Napoleon Bonaparte who was planning to expand his empire. Napoleon offered a 12,000 franc cash prize to anyone who could devise a new practical method for food preservation for armies on the march. A French confectioner and former chef named Nicholas Appert responded to the challenge. After years of experimentation, Appert found a way to preserve food in glass containers. He won the prize in 1810. That same year, fellow Frenchman Pierre Durand patented his own method, only this time using a tin receptacle, and thus creating the modern day process of canning foods. Around the same time, in 1805 in Philadelphia, American inventor Oliver Evans invented the first refrigeration machine. In the decades that followed, both canning and refrigeration technologies gradually improved to the point that by the middle of the 19th century food preservation no longer required salt. Today, we still use and import salt – in fact we import more salt today than in any other period in history – but most readers don't really care who the world's big salt reserve holders are, and whether or how much salt the United States imports. If we have a salt dependency problem, we are more likely to hear about it from our cardiologist than from our president.

The reason we care so much about oil and are sometimes willing to side with unsavory dictators and fight for it is because oil-based fuels presently face no substitutes in the sector in which they are used most – transportation. Transportation underlies our very way of life and indeed the to and fro of people and goods that undergirds the global economy. Oil is therefore a strategic commodity.

Compare oil to another commodity: cocoa. Almost all of the cocoa that makes our chocolate bars, kisses, and drinks is imported, but in early 2011 when violence erupted in Ivory Coast, home to one third of the world's cocoa production, Americans paid little attention. When cocoa prices go up we may eat a bit less and candy makers may lose some money, but the impact to our economy and way of life doesn't even rise to the level of a rounding error (fellow choco-holics, we feel your pain, but keep things in perspective). Even though cocoa prices spiked by nearly 30 percent as Ivory Coast descended into violence, no one called for our military to be deployed to protect the country's cocoa plantations. But the United States and its allies did use force in an insurgency that took place at the exact same time 1,500 miles to the northeast, in Libya. The reason is that, as important as chocolate is in our lives, it is one of many food items on our diet. So if a cup of cocoa becomes too expensive, we can easily settle for coffee or tea instead. The same cannot be said about crude oil, the commodity Libya produces. Before the fall of the Qaddafi regime, Libya was the world's 17th largest oil producer, producing less than two percent of the world's oil. Yet, despite the country's relatively minor production capacity, Libya produces light sweet oil which is uniquely important to the global economy. Sweet oil is the type of crude that is low in sulfur and hence most suitable for the production of gasoline, diesel and jet fuel. Many refineries around the world, primarily in Europe and Asia, are designed to process only sweet crude and are not able to refine the sour crude that comprises most of Saudi Arabia's spare production capacity. As a result, the Libyan insurgency caused the eighth worst oil supply disruption in history, even worse than the 2003 Iraq War. Between mid-February and April 2011 oil prices rose by 25 dollars per barrel.

Oil is a crucial component in the production of every product from toothpaste to golf balls. But most importantly, it comprises 96 percent of our transportation energy. Think about it: almost all of our cars and trucks that enable our 21st century lifestyle can run on nothing but oil. When we buy a new car, in most cases the manual reads something like: "Use only unleaded fuel or unleaded fuel blended with a maximum of 10 percent ethanol. Do not use fuel ethanol (E85), diesel, methanol, leaded fuel or any other fuel." Our cars and trucks are shut off from fuel competition so we can't switch fuel on the fly when oil prices go up. This allows the cartel that dominates the world's oil reserves to collectively act as a monopolist not just in the global oil market but in the global transportation fuel market and thus to have a kind of veto power over global commerce. It is the petroleum-only vehicle that guarantees that oil maintains its status as a strategic commodity to the detriment of our economy and national security. It is the petroleum-only vehicle that gives the oil exporting governments of Saudi Arabia, Iran, Venezuela and Russia inordinate power on the world stage. It is the petroleum-only vehicle that forces us to pay more and more per barrel, sinking our economy deeper and deeper into debt. It is the petroleum-only vehicle that forces us to borrow ever growing amounts of money from China to finance our oil expenditures.

Because the oil market is dominated by a cartel, the petroleum-only vehicle creates a market distortion that begs for correction. Because cars are blocked to fuel competition, oil is not substitutable. If it were, consumers would shift on the fly to competing fuels when oil prices become too high, just choosing to buy something less expensive with which to fuel their cars. How do we know? This is exactly what happened in Brazil. Since the 1973 Arab Oil Embargo, the Brazilians have massively expanded their sugar-based alcohol industry. With warm temperatures and a long rainy season, Brazil has the perfect climate for growing sugarcane. Since 2004, Brazilian drivers have mostly purchased flexible fuel vehicles (FFV) that can run on any combination of gasoline and alcohol. (As we shall soon see, alcohol does not mean just ethanol, and ethanol does not mean just corn.) In 2008, 90 percent of the new cars sold in Brazil were FFVs, many made by General Motors and Ford, and FFVs made up one third of the country's active automobile fleet.[19] What Brazil's flex fuel renaissance did was open the once petroleum dominated transportation fuel market to competition. Ten percent of Brazil's auto fleet, more than 1.5 million cars, can run on natural gas. Most of these natural gas enabled cars are also FFVs. Such tri-fuel cars can run on gasoline, alcohol *and* natural gas. With so many of their cars capable of running on something other than petroleum, Brazilians were able to choose between gasoline, natural gas and alcohol at the pump. This came in handy between 2005 and 2008 when fuel prices nearly doubled elsewhere. When oil prices reached their peak in 2008, ethanol and natural gas became so popular in Brazil that in some parts of the country, including Brazil's largest state of São Paulo, gasoline became an alternative fuel.[20] Now that's energy security.

Drilling and dieting: Two sides of the same coin

The reason it is so important to define the root of our predicament – the petroleum-only vehicle – is because our long held national obsession with imports has led us to waste decades debating policies that are equally irrelevant to the problem. Like two groups of dermatologists arguing whether to apply antibiotics or hormones to a patient with a skin disorder when the real cause of the affliction is bad nutrition, Democrats and Republicans have been debating feverishly whether we should drill more oil or learn to use less of it. To this day, both camps are heavily invested, ideologically, emotionally and financially, in their preferred approach. Drilling and dieting have become political hot buttons by which Republicans and Democrats differentiate themselves (with regional exceptions.) Very few Republican leaders champion dieting and equally few Democrats support unfettered drilling.

From an economic standpoint, there are non-trivial fiscal advantages to producing more oil domestically and deploying technologies that allow us to travel longer distances on a gallon of fuel (as long as their price is reasonable enough to make the math work.) Every dollar of our oil bill that stays in the United States instead of migrating overseas feeds the economy, shrinks our trade deficit and enriches our depleted federal and state coffers, hence slowing of the increase of the federal deficit. Fuel efficient cars also reduce the amount of asthma causing pollutants our cars release to the air. But let's not kid ourselves: these tactics do next to nothing to impact the global price of crude, insulate the economy from perilous oil shocks or reduce the price of gasoline at the pump. They also do nothing to deplete the coffers of our enemies.

Imagine American voters placed a driller-in-chief in the White House who embarked on an all-out drilling campaign, removing every governmental roadblock to seeding Alaska and the Gulf of Mexico with a thousand new rigs, opening tens of thousands of capped wells throughout the continental United States, and developing oil shale formations from Eagle Ford in Texas to the Bakken in North Dakota. Suppose all of this happened and the United States magically became self-sufficient in oil. So self-sufficient that it didn't even have to import oil from Canada. Would that bring down the global price of oil? Would that cut OPEC's revenues? Would that insulate the U.S. economy from price shocks? Would that insulate America's trading partners and serve to guarantee that the products we buy from them do not become costlier? The answer to all of those questions is a resounding no. The reason is that oil is a fungible commodity with a global price. Think of the oil market as a swimming pool: producers pour oil in, consumers take oil out. When the price of oil spikes, it spikes for everyone. A significant disruption in supply from an exporting country affects the entire market, not just its direct clients. Conversely, if a foreign supplier decided to target a specific importer, say the United States, it would fail because the oil will be sold on the markets to the highest bidder, whoever that may be. It is therefore irrelevant whether the United States acquires its oil from domestic or foreign wells. The reality is that even if we did not import a drop of oil — or if all, instead of just most, of our imports came from Canada and Mexico — we'd still be vulnerable to the whims of the oil market and price manipulation by the major oil exporting governments. In 2008, the United Kingdom produced almost all of the oil it needed, yet that didn't stop frustrated truckers from launching a wave of protests to demonstrate against skyrocketing fuel prices. British motorists were affected by the rising price of oil as much as their non-British peers. As mentioned before, only ten percent of our oil supply comes from the Persian Gulf. Yet, our economy has always been – and barring change will continue to be – affected by spikes in oil prices caused by the Persian Gulf's periodic combustions.

As long as oil faces no competition, oil prices will surely go up even if the Mid-East becomes as stable as the Midwest. Why? Because even if we learned how to use less oil, we would never be able to drill enough to offset the rise in demand emanating from developing Asia, and it is not in the interest of the OPEC cartel to expand capacity sufficiently to offset that demand comfortably or even at all. In 1970, the United States produced 9.6 million b/d. In 2011, we produced just over 5.5 million b/d. This means that in just four decades we have lost nearly 40 percent of our total production. With all the drilling activity that is currently taking place domestically, United States' petroleum output could reach 7 million b/d by 2020, perhaps even 10 million b/d at some point. Bringing online millions of barrels of domestic product is an urgent and essential mission. Such a ramp up, even with the most oil friendly administration, would require the oil industry to nearly double in capacity, a monumental task that will take many years and hundreds of billions of dollars to accomplish. But even if such fantastic growth were possible, it would barely cover a third of the growth in demand of developing Asia. China's oil demand is projected to grow from 10 million b/d today to 15 million b/d by 2020. India's demand will grow from 4 to 7 million b/d, and the rest of the developing world will need another one million b/d. In total, 9 million new barrels per day, another Saudi Arabia, would have to come online in just a few years in order to keep oil prices at bay. So should we drill domestically? Absolutely. Would that be enough to drive down crude prices? Absolutely not.

Equally inadequate is the push for an oil diet. Many economists and pundits, as in the above analysis by Michael Mandelbaum, hold that if we just taxed gasoline higher, that would drive down demand and force the automakers to market more fuel efficient vehicles. Interestingly, the voices of gas tax proponents, from liberal Thomas Friedman to conservatives like Charles Krauthammer, are always heard loudest when fuel prices are painfully high. It is then that they come to the rescue, offering to alleviate the pain at the pump by slapping another hefty tax on hardworking American families. Technically the gas-tax proponents are correct. When the price of a product increases, consumers buy less of it. It's true for cocoa; it's true for milk and it's even true for gasoline. The difference is in the degree of those goods' elasticity of demand. The more strategic and less substitutable a commodity or a product is, the less responsive its demand will be to changes in price. Gasoline is one of the least elastic purchases in our consumption basket. The Congressional Budget Office examined consumers response to rising gas prices, concluding that a 10 percent increase in the price of gasoline reduces consumption by merely 0.6 percent and decreases vehicle miles traveled (VMT) by 0.2-0.3 percent. Over the long run, as people replace their vehicles and assuming high gas prices are permanent, the impact grows to 4 percent and VMT drop by 1.1-1.15 percent.[21] In order to demonstrate how limited the effectiveness of gas taxes is, let's examine its implementation in the most extreme case. No country has implemented as sharp an overnight increase in fuel prices in recent history as Iran.

Historically, heavy domestic subsidies for gasoline prices imposed a heavy budget burden on the Iranian government. But with the economic sanctions making the importation of gasoline increasingly difficult, reducing the demand for fuel became a strategic imperative. In December 2010, Iran announced a steep reduction in gasoline subsidies resulting in a 400 percent price increase for the subsidized allocation and a 75 percent price rise for unrestricted purchases. In the year that followed, fuel consumption in Iran fell by merely 8 percent.[22] No serious gasoline tax proponent would advocate such an Iran style radical increase in gasoline tax in the United States, but even if such a policy were politically feasible its results would be profoundly disappointing. As we all know, it isn't. A gasoline tax may sound like a good idea to pundits, but they don't run for election; on the floor of the United States Congress, and arguably in the minds of most Americans, it is blasphemous.

The alternative approach of consumption reduction is a gradual increase of Corporate Average Fuel Economy (CAFE) standards. Unlike gasoline taxes, fuel efficiency has gained great momentum in recent years. The rules initiated by the George W. Bush administration and issued by the Obama administration in April 2010 require automakers to raise fleet wide fuel efficiency from 27 mpg to 35.5 mpg by 2016, and in November 2011 the Obama Administration lifted mandatory fuel economy standards even further to 54.5 miles per gallon by 2025. Increased fuel economy standards would yield cars that run more miles on a gallon of gasoline, which is nice as long as the increase in a vehicle's price to achieve that efficiency doesn't offset the money saved in fuel, but this policy does not address the no-competition-allowed fuel tank. As Table 1 shows, in an environment of rising oil prices, the impact of CAFE standards on our wallet is almost zero and perhaps even a net cost increase if we count the vehicle side cost of increasing efficiency. Efficiency proponents argue that using less will drive prices down, but as long as that reduced U.S. demand is offset — whether by demand growth in the developing world or by an OPEC supply cut - that will not happen.

Table 1: How effective is CAFE in saving you money?

Year	2012	2016	2025
Oil price	$100	$150	$170
$/Gallon/Gasoline	$4	$5	$7.5
MPG	27.6	35.5	54.5
Cents per mile	14	14	14

Under current CAFE rules and at $4 gasoline, consumers pay roughly 14 cents per mile driven. If the price of gasoline remained at $4 a gallon over the next five years, consumers would indeed gain almost three cents per each mile they drive. But if nominal oil prices reach roughly $150 a barrel, a realistic assumption considering the looming inflationary pressures facing our economy, gas prices would climb to $5 a gallon and consumers would pay the exact amount per mile driven they pay today. The same is true for the increase to 54.5 miles per gallon by 2025. If oil prices in 2025 reach, say, $170 a barrel, retail gasoline prices will hover around $7.5, which means the cost per mile driven will remain 14 cents, similar to todays. Putting aside the fact that the recent increase in CAFE standards raises the price tag of new automobiles by more than $2,000 on average, consumers will benefit from this efficiency jump financially only if gasoline prices remain stagnant.[23] But barring a mechanism that keeps the price of oil at bay, the rise in crude prices is likely to erode any purported saving on fuel due to CAFE. As we will show in the next chapter, in all likelihood OPEC's price projections for the third decade of the 21st century will materialize. By then, many of us will drive highly efficient cars. What is far less certain is that such efficiency will leave more money in our pockets.

OPEC, OPEC, OPEC

The reason why drilling and efficiency will not do the trick is OPEC. Members of the cartel sit on 78 percent of world conventional oil reserves, but they account for only one third of global oil production due to a deliberate strategy of constraining supply. One can argue – and many have – that OPEC isn't particularly adept at managing its response to fluctuations in the oil market month to month or week to week. But this is simply unarguable: if investor-owned oil companies such as Exxon, BP, Shell, and Chevron were sitting on top of 78 percent of the world's conventional oil reserves, they wouldn't account for but a third of global supply. They'd probably account for 68 percent, or 82 percent, or something in the ballpark. And if not, they'd be slapped with an anti-trust lawsuit. Anti-trust lawsuits, however, don't work against sovereign regimes that comprise OPEC.

In 1973, just before the Arab Oil Embargo, the oil cartel produced 30 million barrels per day. Forty years later, with global oil demand and non-OPEC production nearly doubling – and despite the fact that in 2007 the cartel inducted two new members, Angola and Ecuador, with combined daily production capacity equivalent to that of Norway[24] – OPEC's crude production has barely increased. Experience of the past three decades clearly shows that whenever non-OPEC producers like the United States increase their production or decrease demand through efficiency, OPEC decreases supply accordingly, keeping the overall amount of oil in the market the same. The reason for this is clear: OPEC countries do not innovate or manufacture much besides oil. They are largely rentier states where citizens pay no income tax. As we explain in Chapter 1, to keep their people content, especially since the Arab Spring, they must generate sufficient revenues to shower them with petrodollars. Since oil is their only export sector, they must keep the price high enough to balance their budgets. And we pay the price twice: once to buy the oil and twice to pay for the direct and indirect costs associated with maintaining a corrupt and unproductive social system which breeds instability and radical ideologies. OPEC's manipulation of oil prices by fluctuating supply is designed for one end: maintaining its collective position as a monopolist not just in the oil market but in the global transportation fuel market.

Strategically, domestic drilling and dieting are two sides of the same coin. They are trivial for a cartel to counter and they do nothing to break oil's virtual monopoly over transportation fuels and thus reduce its strategic importance. To be sure, these policies could keep some of our dollars from migrating overseas, but they have no impact on the global price of crude. As a cartel controlling most of the world's conventional reserves, OPEC can adjust its production down to counter any of our moves. According to the Obama administration, full compliance with the new CAFE standards would yield an annual fuel saving equivalent to

2.2 million b/d by 2025. How difficult would it be for OPEC to sit on its hands and not increase production capacity over the same period of time to keep prices up as the developing world sucks up the oil freed up from American demand? How many times have you heard claims like this?

- "With increased American oil production, world oil prices will also be restrained. [...] This will curtail the huge influx of money currently pouring into oil producing rogue states like Iran." (Newt Gingrich)[25]

  "Lower U.S. consumption could reduce the international price of oil, which would decrease the funds flowing to the governments that depend heavily on oil revenue to finance policies unfriendly to the U.S." (Michael Mandelbaum)[26]

  "A gas tax [...] dries up funding for terrorists and reduces the clout of Iran and Russia." (Tom Friedman)[27]

  "The point of a high U.S. gas tax is to suppress domestic demand and thus suppress the world price." (Charles Krauthammer)[28]

When you hear the pundits and politicians, remember the golden rule: *When we drill more, OPEC can drill less, and when we use less, OPEC also can drill less.* In each of those cases we end up paying more, and they end up raking in more. It follows, then, that the policy options we ought to consider differ significantly from those of the past half-century. Yet there seems to be something seriously the matter with our mental clutch. We're stuck in the wrong gear, and we're not getting anywhere. That needs to change, now.

Needed: an open and competitive fuel market

Over the past seven years in which our oil imports dropped, more than 100 million new petroleum-only vehicles rolled onto America's roads. China, for its part, added 77 million. Since the average lifespan of an American car is 15 years, we effectively extended the stronghold of the oil cartel over our economy by two full decades, and as long as this is the case, we will not be able to ensure our security and prosperity regardless of how much we expand domestic supply or shrink our demand. If tomorrow prices of oil were to climb to well over $200 a barrel due to the collapse of the House of Saud, war between Sunnis and Shiites in the Persian Gulf or a civil war in Algeria or Nigeria – all plausible scenarios – the petroleum-only vehicle would force us to pay insanely high fuel prices in order to get to our workplace, if we still have one. To dial back our debt and insulate our economy from devastating yet inevitable oil price shocks, we must stop acting like a patient asking his physician to administer stronger and stronger medications without realizing that his medical problem was misdiagnosed. Instead, at a time of precarious economic conditions, we should look at the issue through a new lens: courts can't beat the oil cartel but the market can. A competitive market in which different fuels compete over market share would pit oil against fuels made from other energy commodities like natural gas, coal, biomass and so forth. If oil prices become unaffordable, consumers could switch at will to substitute fuels, saving themselves money while forcing oil prices down. Such a competitive environment already exists more or less in our electricity system. Our electric grid is agnostic as to the type of energy that is used to generate power. It is irrelevant to your light bulb whether the electrons powering it were generated from coal, nuclear or solar power. If the price of any of the sources of energy used for power generation were to sharply rise, utilities would find ways to shift to cheaper sources without any adaptation to the grid or to your appliances.

Speaking of the grid, one of the biggest misconceptions in our energy discourse is that our dependence on oil can be mitigated through a shift to electricity sources like nuclear power, solar and wind. We have heard this fallacy from presidential candidates, senators, congressmen, pundits, talking heads and other energy mavens. Let us be clear: today, only one percent of America's electricity is generated from oil, and conversely only about one percent of our oil demand is due to electricity generation. Invoking solar, wind and nuclear power as remedies to oil dependence is like offering Prozac to a cancer patient. Those sources of electricity have nothing – nothing – to do with oil. Build as many nuclear power plants, wind farms and solar arrays as you wish. They might displace coal or natural gas – not oil. Even if magically all the cars in the United States today were plug-in hybrid or electric vehicles, there is enough off peak reserve capacity in the electricity grid to charge the batteries of over 70 percent of the fleet with 99 percent non-oil based power. And the same will be true in the future, as power generation capacity – and with it off-peak reserve capacity – is expanded for reasons having nothing to do with transportation such as new large server farms or increasing demand for plasma TVs.

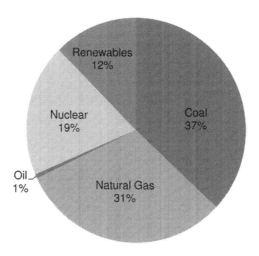

Sources of electric generation in the U.S., 2012

Three musts for competition

For fuel competition to take place in the transportation sector, three conditions must be met. First, the economics of substitute fuels need to make sense: non-petroleum fuels must be able to compete with gasoline and diesel on cost-per-mile driven without any subsidy. Second, the economics of fuel competitive cars need to make sense without complicated net present value calculations that assume a driver owns a car for longer than the average driver does. That means a sticker price close to that of currently available no-fuel-competition vehicles. Asking Americans to fork over thousands of dollars extra at the dealership or for Congress to subsidize millions of cars to the tune of thousands of dollars per unit is a losing proposition. Third, the economics of the distribution infrastructure for substitute fuels must make sense. That means the cost of any needed retrofits to the existing infrastructure or new installations need to need to make business sense to the fuel supply chain and fuel retailers. In the coming chapters we argue that all three conditions can be met in a fiscally conservative way and through a market oriented policy that does not pick winners and does not impose a financial burden on tax payers. It's called the Open Fuel Standard (OFS).

The Open Fuel Standard would break oil's virtual monopoly over the transportation fuel sector by ensuring new cars are not blocked to fuel competition. A number of vehicle technologies offer fuel choice today, including plug-in hybrid electric cars and dual fuel vehicles which run on gasoline and compressed natural gas (CNG), but the simplest and cheapest way to open the fuel market to competition in the near term – with an incremental cost of roughly $100 a car – is by making cars with internal combustion engines liquid fuel flexible, so they are open to any combination of gasoline and alcohol fuels such as methanol and ethanol. Ethanol skeptics and haters: please bear with us. We do not and did not support ethanol subsidies, tariffs, or Soviet central planning style protected markets. In Chapter 7 we distinguish between notorious ethanol policies and the merits of ethanol as a transportation fuel worthy of competing against oil in a free market system. Don't let justified distaste and anger at wasteful and protectionist government policies color your view of a particular fuel or technology. In Chapters 5 and 6 we introduce a little known fuel option, methanol, an unsubsidized, cost effective, and high octane fuel that could relatively quickly take advantage of the cheap natural gas with which the United States is blessed.

This market oriented and fiscally conservative approach that we have been advocating for over a decade has been met by strong opposition from defenders of the status quo of which there are many. Some of the detractors do so for good reason. After all, competition is never welcomed by those in command of the market. We have no illusions. Those who stand to lose from the introduction of fuel competition will never be swayed. This book is not directed toward them but toward the rest of us who believe in the power of markets and free enterprise, the illegitimacy of monopolies and cartels and the right of every American to choose among fuels just as we have choice in every other product we buy.

1

CARTEL AND BARREL:
WHY OPEC *DOES* MATTER

How much does it cost for Saudi Arabia to produce one barrel of oil?
Very little, probably less than $2 to produce a barrel.

Lesley Stahl's 60 Minutes interview
with Saudi Oil Minister Ali al-Naimi, December 2008.[1]

If it takes only $2, the price of a ride on a Manhattan subway, to extract a barrel of oil in Saudi Arabia then why do we pay $100? What's the extra $98 about? Could it be that the Saudis are price gouging? The debate about who is to blame for high oil prices has turned into a national sport. Wall Street, "Big Oil," OPEC, the Federal Reserve's "quantitative easing" programs, Republicans, Democrats, environmentalists, refiners, the Environmental Protection Agency, China and the Big Three automakers have all been accused of pinching hardworking Americans at the pump. In truth, all of the above have something to do – directly or indirectly – with the total cost of our fuel. And while one can try to tease out one reason or another for price shifts at any given point in time, over the long run the best predictor of the price of oil is what we call the breakeven factor.

The breakeven factor

Laid up in New York recovering from a back injury in January 2011, 86-year old King Abdullah of Saudi Arabia was alarmed. Throughout the Middle East, Sunni regimes were crumbling one by one. First Tunisia, then Egypt followed by Libya. Dictators who ruled their countries for decades were forced to resign by angry protestors. If the Egyptian sphinx Hosni Mubarak could be toppled, nobody was immune. What was soon to be known as the "Arab Spring" was engulfing the Arabian Peninsula, and Abdullah was concerned the conflagration would spread to his domain. In Yemen, tens of thousands of protestors demanded the ousting of President Abdullah Saleh and his family who had been in power for 43 years. Hundreds of thousands of mostly Shiite protestors threatened the regime of the Al-Kalifa family in Bahrain. Despite his medical condition, the Saudi King rushed back to Riyadh, and in an attempt to dissuade his subjects from storming the palaces, he showered them with money. Among the measures he announced were outright grants, an increase in subsidies for fuel, foodstuffs, and other goods, a 15 percent raise to all government employees (the vast majority of Saudi workers get a paycheck from the regime) and housing benefits for the military and the Wahhabi religious establishment in exchange for their support of his ban on protests. Altogether $129 billion dollars were committed. This eye popping amount is equivalent to 83 percent of the Kingdom's $154 billion 2011 budget approved before the riots. (For the sake of comparison, the $787 billion economic stimulus plan implemented by the Obama administration constituted a 25 percent bump up in the federal budget.) Saudi Arabia is not the only country where money was used to pacify disgruntled Arabs. Kuwait's Emir Sheikh Ahmad Al Sabah increased his country's budget liabilities by nearly 10 percent, committing to provide each of the country's 1.12 million citizens a grant of $4,000 or $4 billion in total. In addition, he offered nationals free essential foodstuffs for one year at the cost of $1 billion as well as an increase of subsidies for certain food staples. In the United Arab Emirates (UAE) economic incentives announced so far include new subsidies on bread and rice, a promise of an increase in military pensions by 70 percent, and a pledge of $1.9 billion in housing loans. The Qatari regime pledged a package of $8.1 billion including salary hikes in both the public and private sectors and an increase in pensions as well as benefits for the private sector workforce. All government employees got an overnight raise of 60 percent. Soldiers and police salaries soared by 120 percent.

Guess who's footing the bill? Like it or not, the bill for keeping the Persian Gulf monarchies in power is now being footed by oil consumers around the world, including in the U.S.

Countries like Saudi Arabia or Kuwait are called rentier states – states that derive most of their national revenues from the rent of their indigenous resources. There is no personal income tax, no property tax, no sales tax, and no value added tax. Unless you are a foreign company there is also no corporate tax. Additionally, those countries are characterized by bloated public sectors: most people work for Uncle Abdullah. In Saudi Arabia, where roughly 75 percent of the Saudi budget revenues and 90 percent of export earnings come from oil, the public sector currently provides approximately 80 percent of the total employment of Saudi nationals.[2] (According to international standards, public sector employees

should be between 5 percent and 9 percent of the country's workforce.)
Average private sector wages are roughly a third of public sector wages,
creating a strong incentive for Saudis to seek cozy government jobs. In
Iraq, oil accounts for 90 percent of the government's revenues. The number of Iraqis employed in the public sector has doubled between 2005
and 2011, with the public sector currently providing 43 percent of all
jobs and almost 60 percent of all full-time employment.[3] Other OPEC
members present the same situation: Seventy percent of Iran's economy
is state owned, and 90 percent of the Kuwaiti labor force works for the
public sector. Like cancer spreading in a body, high public sector salaries
and benefits not only drain the public budget they also reduce the flow
of money into investment and development funds. In other words: more
government today; less future tomorrow. In the absence of any source
of income other than petrodollars, the government must generate ever
growing revenues from the oil sector and the only way it can do so is by
jacking up oil prices though tight supply.

For years, the Saudis have calibrated oil prices in such a way that oil
revenues are sufficient to balance their budget and ensure cradle-to-grave
services to their booming population. In some years, when oil revenues
surpassed the regime's actual expenditures and the Saudis enjoyed budget surpluses, there was room for largesse and the Saudis released more
oil into the market. At other times, they were willing to coast through
short periods of lower prices in order to achieve a geopolitical objective,
like weakening a competitor or an enemy: Russia (1980s) or Iraq (1990s)
or Iran (today). But in years in which oil prices were too low for comfort
or when government expenditures soared, the Saudis resorted to their
easy solution: tightening of crude export. Consider the experience of the
past few years: between 2005 and 2012 the Saudi budget doubled in size.
What happened to the breakeven price of oil? In 2005, it was $35. In
2008, the International Monetary Fund calculated it was $49 a barrel.[4]
The following year, with the collapse of oil prices, the number jumped
to $75 and in 2011 it stood at $88. The expensive response to the Arab
Spring has already jacked up the breakeven price even further. Merrill
Lynch saw the 2011 break-even price at $95 a barrel, projecting it to
reach $110 in 2015.[5] Now, guess what happened to the global price of
crude over the same period of time? It followed more or less the same
trajectory. Indeed, no predictor of the price of oil and no algorithm con-
cocted by a Wall Street wizard could foretell the price of oil better than
following the budgetary needs of Saudi Arabia.

Table 1.1: Saudi Arabia's budget liabilities and breakeven oil price

Year	Saudi budget ($b)	Actual spending ($b)	Breakeven price to balance actual spending	Average oil price	OPEC production (mb/d)
2005	$74	$92	$35	$50	30.6
2006	$89	$109	$40	$58	30.5
2007	$101	$124	$43	$64	30.1
2008	$109	$138	$49	$91	30.2
2009	$127	$146	$75	$53	28.7
2010	$144	$167	$72	$71	29.2
2011	$154	$223	$88	$87	29.8
2012	$184		$95	$100	31.0

Sources: International Monetary Fund, Jadwa Investment, OPEC

This logic can tell us a lot about where oil prices are headed. The Saudi birth rate is among the highest in the world, and the population, currently at 28 million, is projected to grow by 25 percent by 2025 and by 75 percent by 2050.[6] With 40 percent of the population under the age of 15, a growing number of Saudi youth will enter the job market every year, and the public sector will continue to struggle to absorb incoming fresh graduates. This means that when budgetary requirements grow, so does the need for petrodollars. For the House of Saud, generating ever growing oil revenues will be a matter of do or die. The Riyadh-based Jadwa investments, one of the world most important knowledge bases on the Saudi economy - founded by Prince Faisal Bin Salman Bin Abdulaziz who serves as its chairman - provides an unsettling forecast. According to Jadwa, due to the Arab Spring commitments, the Saudi economy will slide into deficit as early as 2014. This deficit will initially be financed by the cash reserves of the Saudi Arabian Monetary Agency (SAMA), the Kingdom's central bank. But once those cash reserves deplete, the country will have to increasingly finance its budgetary needs with debt and higher per barrel oil prices. According to Jadwa, based on Saudi Arabia's current spending patterns, the breakeven price will rise from its current level to an astronomical $175.1 a barrel in 2025 and a stratospheric $321.7 by 2030.[7]

Table 1.2: Saudi breakeven oil forecast at current spending level

Year	2005	2010	2015	2020	2025	2030
Oil production (mb/d)	9.4	8.2	9.3	10	10.7	11.5
Oil exports (mb/d)	7.5	5.8	6.3	6	5.6	4.9
Domestic consumption (mb/d)	1.9	2.4	3.1	3.9	5.1	6.5
Total revenues (SR billion)	564	735	843	961	1,108	1,120
Total expenditures (SR billion)	346	627	893	1,147	1,620	2,453
Balance (SR billion)	218	109	-50	-186	-512	-1,334
Saudi Arabia Monetary Agency's net foreign assets (SR billion)	564	1,652	1,958	1,331	375	375
Domestic debt (SR billion)	475	167	167	167	949	5,889
Breakeven oil price	$30.3	$71.6	$90.7	$118.5	$175.1	$321.7

Source: Jadwa Investments

An additional, hardly noticed, reason for the inevitable spike in the breakeven price of oil is the decline in Saudi export capacity. This is caused less by geology and more by the country's consumption habits. Everyone knows that Saudi Arabia is the world's largest oil exporter, but the Desert Kingdom is also the world's sixth – yes, sixth – largest oil consumer, surpassing big industrialized countries like Canada, France, Germany, Australia and South Korea. In 2010, Saudi Arabia's per capita annual oil consumption was 38 barrels, almost twice that of the U.S.' Countries of similar population size like Malaysia and Uzbekistan registered per capita oil consumption of 7 and 1.3 barrels respectively. In part due to its natural growth and in part due to heavy subsidization of fuels – Saudi Arabia spends more money on subsidies than on infrastructure development – domestic consumption grows at an annual rate of 7-9 percent. As author Jim Krane put it: "The ruling sheikhs have cemented themselves in power by erecting energy-driven welfare states which provide some of the world's cheapest electricity, natural gas and gasoline."[8] As a result, domestic oil use grew from 1.6 million b/d in 2003 to 2.8 million b/d in 2011. At the current growth rate, Saudi Arabia will consume roughly 6 million b/d by 2030.[9] At its current consumption rate Saudi Arabia will exhaust its spare production capacity before 2020, and oil destined for export will be diverted into the domestic market. Extending the trend even further, before the middle of the century the oil kingdom might become a net oil importer.

Today, Saudi Arabia produces roughly 10 million b/d with production capacity of 12.5 million b/d (that means they could choose to increase production up to their current capacity very rapidly.) Many oil analysts believe that the Saudis don't have the ability to expand production capacity beyond that 12.5 million b/d upper bound. This concern received credence in the writings of oil analysts like the late Matthew Simmons, and has also been expressed by credible Saudi experts. In February 2011, a Wikileaks cable described a November 2007 meeting between the U.S. Consul General in Riyadh and Sadad al-Husseini, a geologist and former head of exploration of Saudi Aramco. In the meeting al-Husseini told the American diplomat that Saudi reserves have been overstated and that Aramco's current production level cannot be sustained.[10] But even if the Saudis did manage to sustain such a high production level a growing portion of their oil will never reach the world market but rather will be consumed domestically.

If the Saudi royals are to maintain the current no-taxation-no-representation social contract they have with their subjects they will have to embark on several politically difficult changes. First, they would have to diversify their economy away from reliance on oil revenues through radical social modifications which entail increasing economic freedom (not the least of which would be full integration of women in the workforce,) and embarking on education and political reforms. Second, they would have to bring domestic demand for petroleum products to a more economic footing through massive cuts in fuel subsidies – Saudis pay 60 cents per gallon of gasoline – and shifting the electricity generation and water desalination sectors from oil to natural gas and solar power. As long as the profit the royals make for exporting an additional barrel of oil is higher than the all-in cost premium for using another power source such as solar to substitute for it for a use such as power generation, they'd be coming out ahead. (Another option, nuclear power, may free the market some oil at the risk of a nuclear Armageddon. The desire to shift to nuclear power by other Gulf regimes has been bizarrely supported by both the Bush and Obama administrations; this may free additional oil for export but we don't see any reason to be more sanguine about radical Sunnis going nuclear than about radical Shia. As we wrote elsewhere, peaceful nuclear power in the context of the Middle East is an oxymoron; at the very least, the U.S. government shouldn't egg it on.)[11] Barring both such social and energy revolutions, the House of Saud is left with one option to balance its budget: drive up oil prices. The Saudis are cognizant that sustained high oil prices fuel political rhetoric about shifting away from oil in the West and if the pain is bad enough and sustained enough run the risk of actually prompting action to trigger a shift to a competitive transportation fuel market. Saudi Prince Al-Waleed bin Talal, one of the world's richest men explained the Saudi conundrum on a CNN interview: "We don't want the West to go and find alternatives, because, clearly, the higher the price of oil goes, the more they have incentives to go and find alternatives."[12] But off the camera, what the Saudis want even less is to end up like the Mubaraks, Ben Alis and Qaddafis of the world. Which is why they will eventually allow the price of oil to crawl up, at times offer 'seasonal discounts,' all while retaining slick PR firms and junk scientists to confuse their clients and instill doubt about the prospects of competing fuels, painting them as environmentally damaging, dangerous or what have you. It is unfortunate that to forward their own political ends, various rabble rousers on the left and right of the U.S. political spectrum on occasion play right into these canards, as we'll discuss in more detail later in the book.

The above dynamic is not unique to Saudi Arabia nor limited to the Gulf monarchies. A similar tale can more or less be applied to Russia, which for the past several years has shared with Saudi Arabia a place on the list of the world's top oil producers. In June 2011, Sergei Ulatov, the resident World Bank economist in Moscow, warned that Russia may face a debt crisis similar to the one gripping Greece by 2030 unless the government reduces spending. "Right now, we are mostly helped by oil prices and not by a very prudent macroeconomic policy," he said.[13] Just like Saudi Arabia, Russia will need high oil (and natural gas) prices to meet its budgetary obligations. Iran, Iraq, Kuwait, Venezuela and Nigeria will all need a higher per barrel oil price as they move toward their rocky future. With a population of 73 million in Iran and 30 million in Iraq, the two countries today need a breakeven price of $125. By 2025 their populations will stand at 88 million and 45 million respectively. Where will the money come from? There is a limit to the amount of money to be made from exporting carpets, dates and pistachio nuts. There is no limit to the amount of revenues to be made from oil exports.

Why OPEC matters

In the summer of 2012 as part of the preparations toward the publication of its issue on energy, *Foreign Policy Magazine* requested 57 energy experts to rank the factors most affecting global oil prices. Among the options offered: oil companies, Wall Street speculators, increasing demand in developing countries, environmental regulations, wars and other human disruptions, economic sanctions, politicians and geological constraints. One factor wasn't even listed on the menu of options: OPEC. It is not surprising that the oil cartel is viewed today by many energy experts as a dysfunctional bunch with diminishing, if any, control over the oil market. Its members are at odds with each other; its product faces growing challenges on multiple fronts from non-conventional oil to electric vehicles; and its spare capacity – the important cushion that for many years protected the oil market from nasty supply disruptions and from which the cartel derived its power and influence – is thinning. Among analysts who perceive themselves as sophisticated, blaming OPEC for the market's dislocations is a sign of intellectual laziness and simple mindedness. "OPEC looks like a masterful cartel when, in fact, it is mainly just riding the waves," *Newsweek* concluded in a 2008 editorial titled "OPEC is Irrelevant."[14] We unapologetically disagree.

Conventional wisdom holds that the problem of oil is one of fundamentals. Simply put: a lot of demand, not enough supply. Many – including 80 percent of the experts surveyed by *Foreign Policy* - see the squeeze driven by powerful economic growth in emerging markets as the driver behind the upward movement in oil prices.[15] Sure enough, Asia's economic growth since the beginning of the 21st century has astounded the world. Hundreds of millions of Chinese, Indians, Indonesians and Vietnamese are rising from poverty and shifting from muscle power to motorized transport. While diesel generators supply power in locales where the electricity grid isn't reliable or in some cases existent, the vast majority of electricity in the developing world is generated from something other than oil, and the new power plants going online daily in China and India are not oil fueled. The developing world's demand for crude is – just as in the developed world - transportation driven. In the first decade of the 21st century China's oil demand more than doubled, and in 2010 China surpassed the United States as the world's largest auto market. India, projected to surpass China by 2025 as the world's most populous country, is following a similar growth trajectory in terms of oil demand.

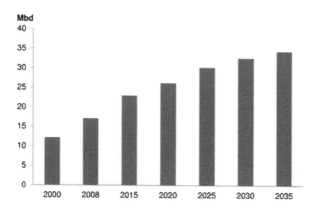

Developing Asia's oil demand projection

Source: International Energy Agency

But Asia's growing demand would not have been enough of a reason for oil prices to increase so sharply if it had been coupled with a parallel growth in supply. We've been there before. In the decade-and-a- half between 1956 and 1973, the U.S. economy grew at an annual rate of 4-6 percent. America became a nation of motorists who took to newly built roads like the New Jersey Turnpike on board cars that ran on cheap gasoline. But just like today, it was Asia where the growth engines roared the loudest. The Japanese economy experienced phenomenal economic growth of 6-12 percent per year, similar to the current growth rate of China and India. Did the rise in global prosperity and in particular that of what was to become the world's second largest economy drive up the price of oil? No. Over that period, during the height of the Cold War and with three major wars in the Middle East, the inflation adjusted price of oil actually fell by 18 percent. In the 1960s, economic growth did not drive up the price of oil, because during most of that period the oil market was controlled by the Seven Sisters – the seven investor owned western oil companies which dominated the global petroleum industry from the mid-1940s to the 1970s. The group, comprised of Standard Oil of New Jersey and Standard Oil Company of New York (now ExxonMobil), Standard Oil of California, Gulf Oil and Texaco (now

Chevron), Royal Dutch Shell, and Anglo-Persian Oil Company (now BP), controlled 85 percent of global reserves. In the 1950s and 1960s, the oil majors spanned the globe and poured huge investments into exploration, recovery, infrastructure and refining operations. In other words, they responded to growing demand as one would expect competing companies to respond: with increased production capacity and more supply. The U.S. alone produced a third of the world oil supply. While the rest of the world celebrated cheap oil, the leaders of Venezuela and the Persian Gulf countries were outraged. They felt the Seven Sisters were exploiting their oil reserves too fast and were not happy about their share of the take. "They kept reducing the price," complained then Saudi Arabia's Oil Minister Ahmed Zaki Yamani, adding "this was not acceptable." In 1960, five of the world's top oil-producing countries spearheaded by Venezuela's oil minister, Perez Alfonso, convened in Baghdad to create a cartel to manage the world oil market. The goal of the newly formed OPEC cartel was to "assert its member countries' legitimate rights" and gain "a major say in the pricing of crude oil on world markets." It did just that. In the decades that followed, unlike the Seven Sisters that did all they could to meet demand, OPEC members nationalized international companies' oil fields and infrastructure assets, instituted a quota system, and gained the upper hand in price negotiations. Within a decade, they had become the most powerful cartel in modern history. As their collective power grew, OPEC members also learned to use oil as an instrument of geopolitical power. Their boldest experiment occurred in 1973, when the cartel's Arab members imposed a five-month oil embargo to deter Western nations from supporting Israel in the Yom Kippur War. They also cut overall production.

Just an embargo to specific countries rather than a curtailment of total production wouldn't have had a significant impact on price because oil is a fungible commodity – think of the oil market as a swimming pool: producers pour oil in, consumers take oil out. So embargoing oil to a specific country would simply cause that country to buy from another supplier, while someone else purchases oil from the embargoing regime. However, an overall cut in supply to a market (in this case the global oil market) will drive prices up unless other producers can meet the shortfall at as low a production cost as the supply cutters. The Arab countries cut production by some 25 percent; and oil prices rose by a factor of four. Lower supply means higher prices mean lower demand. However, artificially keeping the price low for consumers via price controls means demand doesn't fall. Less supply, no drop in demand is a recipe for shortages. And indeed that is what happened. The price rise was the doing of the Arab OPEC members; the bureaucratic response of price controls and rationing in the United States and elsewhere is what caused shortages and long lines at gas pumps.

Since then, OPEC has earned a reputation as a club of sclerotic, non-democratic regimes whose oil ministers gather in Vienna every few months to set the price of crude, holding the world by the you know what. Yoweri Museveni, president of Uganda, recounted the role of Qaddafi, the recently deposed ruler of Libya, in pushing up oil prices: "Before Qaddafi came to power in 1969, a barrel of oil was 40 American cents. He launched a campaign to withhold Arab oil unless the West paid more for it. I think the price went up to $20 per barrel. [...] The huge wealth many of these oil producers are enjoying was, at least in part, due to Qaddafi's efforts."[16] While Qaddafi is at present smelling the daisies by the roots, there are many such characters left in OPEC.

Fireman or arsonist?

Cartels are not a new phenomenon. Throughout history there have been a number of cases in which markets of important goods and commodities were prevented from operating freely. In the early years of the 20th century, the De Beers diamond conglomerate controlled 90 percent of the world's diamond production. The Phoebus cartel, which included companies like Philips and General Electric, controlled the manufacture and sale of light bulbs from 1924 until 1939. Even in today's globalized world several markets of niche products are cartelized, including food additives and preservatives like lysine, citric acid and sorbates, industrial cleaners like sodium gluconate and graphite electrodes used in steel production. The firms and individuals involved are not owned by unsavory dictators in Africa or the Middle East but rather by American, Belgian, Dutch, French, German, Italian, Japanese, and Swiss players. But as explained before, oil is not lysine. In 1910, De Beers Chairman Ernest Oppenheimer explained: "Common sense tells us that the only way to increase the value of diamonds is to make them scarce, that is to reduce production."[17] This is exactly what OPEC has done since the 1970s. Like the other cartels, OPEC has used its dominant position in the international oil market to manipulate the price of its product and hence maximize its members' profits. OPEC's tactics have ranged from scarcity creation, aimed at pushing prices up, to flooding the market with oil when competition becomes a threat. When non-OPEC production increases, OPEC can simply respond with quota cuts to counter the increase, and keep the price intact. Similarly, when consumption drops in the major consuming economies due to austerity measures or a slowdown in growth, OPEC can respond with production cuts.

In 2008, due to the meteoric rise in gasoline prices and the subsequent economic slowdown, U.S. oil demand dropped by nearly one million barrels per day. It was as if the fuel efficiency of the entire U.S. vehicle fleet magically increased by 2.5 miles per gallon overnight. What was OPEC's response? First, it called for an emergency meeting in Vienna in October where it reduced production by 1.5 million b/d. A following meeting in Cairo in November reaffirmed the decision. Then, in December that year, OPEC members met again to reduce production by additional 2.2 million b/d. Altogether OPEC dropped production by roughly 3.5 million b/d which is more than the amount of oil that was actually saved throughout the world due to reduced consumer demand. In 2010, when the economy began to recover and with it global oil demand, OPEC was called to ramp up its production by 1.17 million b/d. It barely provided half of this amount. As a result, crude prices rose by 29 percent. In 2011, OPEC again failed to deliver, increasing output by only 280,000 barrels instead of 470,000 additional barrels the market needed. The cartel's tardiness in replacing Libya's production caused oil prices to rise by another 41 percent.[18]

Table 1.3: OPEC's response to the market's needs (in million b/d)

Year	2009	2010	2011
Oil demand	-1.10	2.57	0.87
Less non-OPEC supply	1.90	1.14	0.73
Less OPEC's NGL	0.02	0.46	0.31
Call on OPEC	-3.01	0.97	-0.17
Less previous year surplus	0.16	-0.20	-0.64
Need from OPEC	-3.18	1.17	0.47
Change in OPEC's output	-3.38	0.53	0.28
% change in crude price	-37	29	41

Like other cartels, OPEC's machinations have gone toward one end: maximizing profits for its members. While OPEC's members squabble about the ideal target price for oil, some aiming super high while others are happy with mildly high, and aren't necessarily particularly adept at responding in sync with production changes in the short term, OPEC has proved adept at keeping its collective production *capacity* much lower than it otherwise would have been. Capacity takes a long time to ramp up and is the upper bound on oil output. A country can always supply less than its capacity permits, but by definition can't supply more unless it invests in expanding its capacity, something that takes time and effort. Since it has been effective at constraining its collective capacity, OPEC has managed to in the big picture overcome the natural problem of a cartel, which is that members tend to lack discipline and cohesion and, striving to maximize their own profits, produce more than they actually agreed to. OPEC members may do that, but only up to the capacity bound. As long as OPEC's collective capacity is lower than would be warranted by its reserves, the cartel is guaranteed that prices will be higher than they would be in a competitive market. Since capacity expansion takes a long time to implement, it's much easier for OPEC to stay disciplined. While sitting on 78 percent of world conventional oil reserves, the cartel accounts for a mere third of global oil supply. The world's non-OPEC producers, America among them, with little more than a fifth of the world's conventional oil at their disposal, pump twice as much. If investor owned companies such as BP, Exxon, Chevron, and Shell controlled 78 percent of global oil reserves like OPEC (in actually they own a mere eight percent and have access to less than a quarter), they would have expanded capacity as global demand increased, just as they did when they were in the catbird seat of the global oil market and accounted for a share of global oil production somewhere in the ballpark of what these reserves allow, which is probably about double of where OPEC is today (assuming the cartel hasn't been lying about its reserve numbers, a non-negligible possibility).

OPEC as a collective essentially holds the position of a monopolist in the global oil market, and - as long as cars are closed to competing fuels – it thus holds the position of a monopolist in the global transportation fuel market. This power enables OPEC to respond to changes in consumer demand and non-OPEC supply in a way that keeps prices high. No matter what non-OPEC countries like the United States do, OPEC always has the upper hand. Just like De Beers flooded the market with diamonds in order to drive competitors out of business, OPEC too has taken aggressive steps to crowd out of the market other oil producers as well as potential competing fuels. Producers of non-conventional crude from tar sands or oil shale are the biggest potential casualties of OPEC's machinations. Since the per barrel production costs of non-conventional crude are substantially higher than those OPEC faces, investors in these firms need certainty that their processes can remain competitive. Fully aware of the vastness of those non-conventional reserves, OPEC periodically drives down crude prices in order to bankrupt producers of non-conventional crude. The same has been true for some non-petroleum fuels.

One reason the world has been willing to tolerate OPEC's manipulation is that the cartel controls almost all the market's spare production capacity -- the main protection the world's economy has against supply disruptions. OPEC is therefore viewed by some as a force for good, pouring product into the market every time disruption occurs. But a closer examination into OPEC's performance as a buffer against oil shocks shows that the cartel has seldom used its vaunted capacity to rescue an oil-starved market. Time and again when disruptions occur, OPEC drags its feet and ignores consumers' pleas to open the spigot and provide some relief. Instead it insists that the market is well-supplied and that high oil prices are the work of speculators and SUV-driving soccer moms. It also adjusts the definition of "fair" price. In 2004, OPEC's "fair" price was $25 a barrel. Two years later, $50 was considered "ideal." In 2010, OPEC's secretary general, Abdalla Salem El-Badri argued for $90, and by the end of 2011, with OPEC's oil revenues topping $1 trillion, he adjusted the price to $100. "The target of $100 is good both for producers, consumers and the oil industry. I think this is a price that is good for everyone. So this is our target," was the message to anguished consumers from Saudi Arabia's Finance Minister Ibrahim Al-Assaf in April 2012.[19] True to form, OPEC never takes responsibility for high oil price. In the wake of the Arab Spring oil disruption in March 2011, Saudi Arabia's al-Naimi deflected the blame to Wall Street, claiming that "crude oil prices are not supported by basic supply-demand balances and have more to do with financial speculation."[20] In close discussions with U.S. diplomats, the Saudis claimed that speculation represented approximately $40 of the overall oil price when it was at its height. Nothing to do with their actions. They sent the U.S. Congress to do homework, demanding that the U.S. impose restrictions on oil trading.[21]

Not only is OPEC not an agent of stability, its members are, in most cases, responsible for the very same supply disruptions they are supposedly interested in countering. They may claim to be the global economy's fireman, but its members have spent more time behaving like arsonists. We have the cartel's members to thank not just for the 1973 embargo, but also for Saddam Hussein's attacks on Iran and Kuwait, Nigeria's endless war in the Niger Delta, the 2003 oil strike in Venezuela, the civil war in Libya and Iran's threats to block the Straits of Hormuz. All of those cost us dearly.

The world economy grows, OPEC production barely

For all its bluster, OPEC seems almost uninterested in actually getting its oil out of the ground. In the past four decades world population grew by 70 percent, global GDP grew fourteen fold, the number of automobiles quadrupled and global oil demand grew by 60 percent. By how much has OPEC's production grown? Despite the 2007 induction of two new members, Angola and Ecuador (Ecuador actually rejoined OPEC in 2007; it had left the organization in 1992,) who collectively produce as much oil each day as Norway, OPEC's current production level is similar to that of four decades ago.

Table 1.4: The world economy grows, OPEC production barely

	1973	2012
World population	4 billion	7 billion
Number of automobiles	250 million	1000 million
World GDP	5 trillion	70 trillion
Global oil demand	55 mb/d	87 mb/d
OPEC production	30 mb/d	31 mb/d
Share of global supply	54%	36%

Source: Institute for the Analysis of Global Security

OPEC clearly produces far less than its reserves allow. This is done intentionally in order to stretch the cartel's power as far as possible into the future. While non-OPEC producers rush to exhaust their reserves, pumping oil at a market responsive pace – Drill-Baby-Drilling, if you will - members of the oil cartel prefer to mothball supply. In 2008, when oil prices were in the stratosphere, new large fields were discovered in Saudi Arabia. King Abdullah ordered that those new finds be left untapped to preserve the nation's oil wealth for future generations. "When there were new finds, I told them, 'No, leave it in the ground, with grace from God, our children need it,'" the king said.[22] Behind the king's statement lies a plain truth: the Saudi reserve-to-production ratio - an indicator of how long proven reserves could last at current production rates - is 70 years; Iran's is 82; the United Arab Emirates' is 90; and Venezuela's is 91. Iraq and Kuwait are at more than 100. The U.S. ratio? Eleven years. We want cheap oil today; the oil exporters need exportable oil tomorrow. Even more important – they need to balance their budget.

Defanging a cartel

Cartels and monopolies reflect a natural tendency of market actors to maximize their profits and limit competition. But this is one of the rare cases where even the most avid free marketers would agree that there is both room and imperative for government to intervene in order to correct the situation. The question remains how. Under the Sherman Anti-Trust Law which outlaws all conspiracies that unreasonably restrain interstate and foreign trade, price collusion is considered a criminal activity, and the U.S. Department of Justice Antitrust Division has embarked on numerous criminal investigations against firms suspected of market rigging, conspiracies and antitrust violations. This law, as well as the Clayton Act which prohibits mergers or acquisitions that are likely to lessen competition, has also been applied in extraterritorial cases – but never against OPEC. Americans may fear the concentration of arbitrary power in the hands of their own politicians. Apparently less so when it comes to foreign ones.

Outside of the U.S., the rules of the World Trade Organization (WTO) contain anti-trust provisions and most OECD countries have strict laws against cartels, monopolies and international mergers that impede competition. But neither U.S. authorities nor the multiple international bodies carrying the banner of free trade have gathered the courage to confront OPEC, the biggest violator of free trade the world has ever seen. To the contrary, on December 11, 2005, the WTO admitted Saudi Arabia, the de facto head of OPEC, as full member. Beyond Saudi Arabia, of the other 11 current OPEC members, seven (Angola, Ecuador, Kuwait, Nigeria, Qatar, the UAE and Venezuela) have already become members of the WTO, and four (Algeria, Libya, Iran and Iraq) are negotiating their terms of accession. Even worse, the most important

WTO Ministerial Conference since its birth in 1995 was hosted by OPEC member Qatar, and the new round of trade negotiations, the Doha Development Round, whose objective is to lower trade barriers around the world, which will help facilitate the increase of global trade, was shamefully named after the conference host city. The U.S. government and justice system too have displayed apathy in the face of OPEC's behavior. About 15 variations of a bill called No Oil Producing and Exporting Cartels Act of 2000 (NOPEC) which seeks to hold OPEC member states liable for violations of U.S. antitrust legislation have been introduced before the U.S. Congress since 1999. All of them were rejected on the grounds of international law's Act of State Doctrine which claims that one nation cannot infringe on the sovereign act of another if it occurs in the latter's territory. Both the Bush and Obama administrations have formally stated their opposition to NOPEC explaining that the adoption of such a law would invoke retaliatory measures against American-held assets abroad. As a result of this feeble response, the U.S. economy remains at the mercy of what commentator Claudia Rosett impolitely defined as "a gang of price-fixing, oil-rich thug regimes that meet to reinforce assorted terrorist-sponsoring tyrants and gouge consumers."

Saudi Arabia accession into the WTO. Free trade indeed.

The reason OPEC members can show indifference to the pain they inflict throughout the globe every time they decide to manipulate oil prices is because we allow them to do so. Very few commodities that cost $2 to produce can be sold for $100, the vendor deems the price to be "fair and reasonable" yet the consumer comes back for more and more. Another reason for OPEC's boldness is that its members know something many in the U.S. still refuse to acknowledge: time is working in their favor. Despite development of oil fields in domains outside OPEC such as West Africa, Russia, Brazil the Caspian and as of recently, the U.S., in the long run OPEC members know that the world's dependence on them will only increase. With global oil demand projected to surpass 100 million b/d in two decades, many of today's non-OPEC producers, including Mexico, Canada, Norway and Russia will deplete their reserves faster than OPEC and reach a point in which they are no longer relevant players in the oil market. At that point the percentage of world conventional oil reserves concentrated in OPEC countries could reach 90 percent in comparison to 78 percent today, and OPEC's share of total oil supply is projected to bounce from 40 percent today to about 60 percent. Beyond that point, OPEC will be able to charge any price for oil – and we will be forced to pay. There is only one way to avoid this course. Outmaneuvering the cartel requires the ability to respond dynamically - on the fly - to price shifts by substituting its product with another good. It's called competition.

2

THE MAKING AND BREAKING OF PETROPOLY

Howard Hughes: Do you think it's fair for one airline to have a monopoly on international travel?

Senator Owen Brewster: I think an airline can do better without competition. All I'm thinking about is the needs of the American passenger.

The Aviator, John Logan

Until the early 20th century the horse was the principal means of transportation in the rapidly growing continental United States. Horse transportation was quite slow over long distances and bad roads. It was also expensive. In urban settings, one had to be fairly well off to own, feed, and house a horse, and those who couldn't made do on foot or took horse-cabs.[1] Rising prices of hay, oats, farming land and veterinary services made the horse increasingly unprofitable – "too costly to buy and too costly to keep."[2] In urban settings, electric streetcars made significant inroads, and rail and steamboats sped up travel significantly for freight and for those who could afford the fare. However, Randal O'Toole estimates that by the end of the 19th century average travel speed had only risen to eight miles per hour. Most people didn't travel very much. This was the scenario onto which automobiles made their debut. "No wonder modern late nineteenth-century society reacted with wonderment and excitement at a new invention," wrote author Edwin Black about the introduction of the vehicle. "This machine [...] could do the work of a team of horses, never slept, and required no feeding. This invention promised to propel humankind into a dazzling new era of possibilities."[3] It did. The number of automobiles in the United States climbed from 8,000 in 1900 to 902,000 in 1912. In that year, New York, London, and Paris traffic counts for the first time all showed more cars than horses.

To the modern reader, a horse is perceived as a friendly and aristocratic creature, but for most Americans of that time, it was a source of an intolerable all-encompassing environmental crisis. The average city horse distributed along the course of its route between 15 and 35 pounds of manure and about a quart of urine every single working day.[4] The manure was everywhere, and an entire industry of dung collectors and recyclers emerged in all the big cities. Those droppings not only raised an intolerable stench but also attracted clouds of flies, contributing to the spread of infectious diseases. During rainy days, city streets became an appalling quagmire. Crossing the street was a nasty experience. In hot days the manure dried up and turned into airborne powder breathable by rich and poor alike. Worse than the living horses were the dead ones. In 1880, some 15,000 horses died on New York streets alone. Getting rid of the corpses became a huge logistical, environmental and financial challenge. Altogether thousands of humans died each year from diseases spread by horse manure and carcasses. But the public health fears were not enough to drive the shift from the horse to the motor vehicle. It was the pocketbook: a better product at a lower price. Present day environmentalists focused on mitigating the environmental downsides of modern life would be well advised to remember that. The car revolution was well on its way, but what the car would run on was still an open question.

The era of fuel choice: 1890-1914

At the beginning of the 20th century, there weren't very many vehicles but there was quite a competition among different vehicle technologies, employing different sources of power. In the three decades prior to World War I, Americans saw a competition among vehicle technologies employing different transportation fuels like it has not seen since. Dozens of car models operated by batteries, steam engines and internal combustion engines competed in the transportation fuels marketplace for the heart and wallet of the American consumer. It was not always free competition – there was intrigue and even foul play – but it was nonetheless competition. Forty percent of American automobiles were powered by steam, 38 percent by electricity, and only 22 percent by liquid fuels.[5] Consumers could choose between noisy, smelly gasoline cars and odorless and noiseless electric vehicles. High speed fans could buy the Stanley steam car, which between 1906 and 1910 was considered the fastest car on the road. But it was Henry Ford who eventually tilted the balance in favor of liquid fuels. On September 27, 1908, the automotive market changed forever when the first Model T left the Ford factory on Detroit's Piquette Avenue. It was the first of 15 million Model T's that would roll onto worldwide roads in the subsequent two decades. In 1913, Ford took a technology that was still a province of the relatively well off into mass production, slashing its price by half. All of a sudden, a person didn't have to be wealthy to travel on his own when and where he wished. Very few machines had as lasting an influence on American society as did the Model T, which ushered in an era of affordable personal motorized mobility for the rapidly growing American middle class.

The famous statement that the public could have a Model T Ford "in any color, so long as it's black," is commonly attributed to Henry Ford. But if the Model T offered little choice in color, it certainly offered choice in fuel. Just like Rudolf Diesel, the inventor of the diesel engine, designed his engine to run on both vegetable oil and petroleum fuel, Henry Ford designed the Model T's four cylinder internal combustion engine to run on gasoline, kerosene and alcohol - a true flexible fuel vehicle. This fuel flexibility aimed to address the needs of rural Americans who had no access to gasoline but could distill alcohol locally to run their cars and farm machinery. Alcohol was operating under a heavy government imposed handicap: in the 1860s, a $2.08 per gallon federal sin tax on alcohol was passed with the purported aim of paying for the Civil War.[6] Alas, the tax did not distinguish between beverage alcohol and fuel alcohol, and at the time of its enactment struck a death blow to the then ubiquitous use of alcohol as a fuel for lamps (in comparison, kerosene was taxed at 10 cents a gallon.) In 1906, as part of his trust busting effort against Standard Oil, President Teddy Roosevelt urged Congress to lift the alcohol tax: "The Standard Oil Company has, largely by unfair or unlawful methods, crushed out home competition. It is highly desirable that an element of competition should be introduced by the passage of some such law as that which has already passed the House, putting alcohol used in the arts and manufactures upon the [tax] free list."[7] The tax was finally rolled back. Without it, alcohol was 30 percent cheaper than gasoline, and it soon became most farmers' fuel of choice. It became even more attractive in the fall of 1912 when gasoline prices soared by 75 percent over the previous year.[8] Gasoline, which 20 years earlier was an almost worthless byproduct of the oil refining industry, became so expensive that one tank of it could easily exceed two days' wages of the average factory worker who assembled such cars. But the pendulum was about to swing back in favor of gasoline; only this time, gathering powerful momentum, it transformed into a wrecking ball.

The crowning of gasoline 1914-1933

The following years gave gasoline the push it needed to demolish all of its competitors and become the omnipresent fuel for the rest of the 20th century. First came the complete abandonment in 1914 of the electric car after Henry Ford and Thomas Edison's ambitious plan to mass produce an electric version of the Model-T was derailed.[9] Then came World War I, which brought about the weaponization of the automobile. Tactical vehicles required fuel that was energy dense yet ubiquitous and easily handled. Of all the fuels of the time, gasoline and diesel were the best fits for battlefield conditions. The next blow to competition with gasoline was the fall from grace of alcohol fuels. The war diverted much of the alcohol to the manufacturing of ammunition and war gases, driving up its price as fuel. In the wake of war came Prohibition. On January 16 1919, the U.S. Senate ratified the Eighteenth Amendment to the Constitution. This amendment required Congress to ban the manufacture, sale or transportation of alcohol throughout U.S. territory. The era of Prohibition, by effectively criminalizing backyard stills and thus the self-production of boozy beverage and fuel by the rural population, reduced the big no-middleman advantage of ethanol and boosted the oil industry's effort to develop a nationwide gasoline refueling infrastructure to meet the needs of the emerging car ownership society. In 1933, concerned about sparking interest in alcohol fuel – particularly as an octane booster that unlike tetraethyl lead was harmless to human health – the American Petroleum Institute issued internal memos urging a coordinated effort to oppose fuel blending, warning that it "will harm the petroleum industry and the automobile industry as well as state and national treasuries by reducing [oil] consumption" and would be lucrative to bootleggers.[10]

Just like every act of infringement on freedoms by government, Prohibition was highly unpopular and became increasingly so as its unintended consequences – rise in crime, organized bootlegging, job loss, and as many as 10,000 unnecessary deaths from drinking denatured alcohol– became apparent to all. When in 1933 the Twenty-First Amendment repealed the Eighteenth Amendment, working Americans rejoiced in their now legal saloons and cocktail bars. There would be no more nasty scenes of liquor barrels destroyed by government agents. But for the fuel market all of this would no longer matter. Gasoline was so deeply entrenched in the marketplace and competitors with it were at such a disadvantage, that there was little incentive for any of them to reemerge.

The era of petropoly: 1933-2005

In the early 1930s, America sank into the Great Depression. Conditions in rural America were the worst as agricultural commodity prices plunged. As if this were not enough, severe droughts in the early 1930s devastated millions of acres of farmland and caused millions to migrate from the dust storms of rural America to the cities. The ordeals of those Dust Bowl victims were memorialized in John Steinbeck's novel the *Grapes of Wrath*. Like those of other commodities, oil prices also tumbled and not only because demand for fuel slowed as automobile sales declined. What sent oil prices to the bottom was expanded supply: major oil discoveries in the late 1920s in Pennsylvania, Oklahoma and California, and, most of all, the 1930 discovery of the East Texas oil field, the largest reservoir in the United States outside of Alaska. In the wake of the new supply, a barrel of Texas crude that was selling for as high as $1.85 in 1926 was priced as low as 15 cents in 1931.[11] The East Texas oil boom of 1930 created fierce, at times violent, competition between oil producers. In their eyes, the price collapse of the early 1930s required a system to control and stabilize oil prices. The Texas Railroad Commission (TRC), the state agency that until that time regulated railroads, terminals and pipelines, was assigned the task of regulating production quotas for Texas oil. The success of President Franklin D. Roosevelt's New Deal depended to a large degree on the health and profitability of America's oil industry. Roosevelt authorized the TRC, which as late as the 1950s controlled over 40 percent of U.S. crude production and approximately half of estimated national proven reserves, to regulate production levels nationally. The TRC was oil-patch based, far from the public eye and could do its job discreetly with less controversy than the federal government out of Washington, DC. Roosevelt's policies also prevented competition with foreign oil. Just like the U.S. imposed a stiff 54 cent per gallon tariff on imported ethanol until 2012, in 1932 a tariff of 21 cents per barrel of foreign crude and 2.5 cents on a gallon of gasoline, equivalent to a 50 cent tariff on today's gasoline, was signed into law.[12] In legitimizing the TRC's practice of withholding product from the market in order to keep oil prices artificially high, FDR wrote the playbook by which OPEC operates today.

The years between the Great Depression and the outbreak of World War II left America's fuel market with very little space to reintroduce fuels competitive with gasoline. When the war started, the U.S. auto industry halted its passenger vehicle production, and assembly lines were converted to produce hundreds of thousands of tanks, jeeps, combat cars and millions of tons of other equipment that ultimately helped the United States win the war. Since quartermasters preferred a simple one-fuel system, these tactical vehicles were designed to run on one ubiquitous and versatile petroleum-based fuel that would be available in every theater of war from Burma to Berlin.

All of these historical circumstances should not mask the most important reason why gasoline prevailed over all other fuels. It was simply a superb fuel which offered a unique optimization between functionality and convenience. It surpassed most fuels in terms of energy density, yet it had sufficiently high octane to provide variable power and rapid acceleration. Most important, from the days it was a worthless byproduct of kerosene for home lighting until not too many years ago, it was too cheap to beat. In the four decades that elapsed between the end of the Depression and the 1973 Arab Oil Embargo gasoline prices never surpassed 50 cents per gallon. Even with the change of management when OPEC seized control over the oil market from the Seven Sisters and the oil crises of the 1970s, the highest price gasoline reached was $1.38. At this level there was simply no room for competition to it. That is to say, the creation of oil's monopoly over transportation fuels was not an act of collusion or conspiracy. It was purely the result of political and economic circumstances. As long as oil prices were low, petroleum fuels were the natural choice for humanity. But from the very beginning of the oil era, as early as 1938, with Mexico's expropriation of American and British oil companies, there were multiple red flags that should have signaled that betting the future of the global transportation sector on one type of fuel, plentiful as it may be, would put America on a perilous path. Iran's 1951 nationalization of the Anglo-Persian Oil Company, Egypt's 1956 nationalization of the Suez Canal, a major conduit of oil shipment through which two thirds of Europe's oil passed daily, the 1960 formation of OPEC, the 1973 Arab Oil Embargo, the Iranian revolution, the subsequent Iran-Iraq War, and the 1990 and 2003 Gulf Wars were just a few of the tell-tale signs that something could go very wrong should America continue to depend on oil as the sole source of energy in the transportation sector. But, as we know from other walks of life, individuals, and governments in particular, are not good at responding to tell-tale signs. Crises came and went and with them America's will to confront petropoly head on.

The new era of choice?

When future historians write the history of our time, we predict they will point out that the years 2005 and 2006 were the watershed years in which humanity began to bounce back from petropoly to a competitive fuel marketplace. Why those years? First, it was the point in time when oil market first indicated that there is no going back to the price levels of $20-$30 a barrel. Oil began its upward move toward a new price plateau, which leveled at roughly $100. To be sure, there is plenty of oil on planet earth, but even the most optimistic industry analysts understand that new supplies of oil, extracted from the deep sea, tar sands, the crevices in shale formations or in the future the kerogen in oil shale itself are orders of magnitude more costly to access and/or refine than Arabian crude. The first decade of the 21st century was also the time the world internalized that the voracious appetite of new transportation fuel consumers like China and India was not going to wane. Even before 2005, China embarked on a global oil exploration frenzy and that had a negative impact on its relations with Washington. As early as 2002, a report by the U.S.-China Economic and Security Review Commission, a group created by Congress to monitor U.S.-China relations, warned that "A key driver in China's relations with terrorist-sponsoring governments is its dependence on foreign oil to fuel its economic development. This dependency is expected to increase over the coming decade."[13] But it was only in the summer of 2005 that the challenge of China's pursuit of oil registered in the American mind when the China National Offshore Oil Corporation, known as CNOOC, offered $18.5 billion for the American oil company Unocal, a bid that was eventually rejected by the U.S. Congress. The year 2005 was also the year Mahmoud Ahmadinejad became the sixth president of Iran. Under his leadership, Iran's support of terrorism and its unflinching commitment to the development of nuclear capabilities could usher the Persian Gulf and indeed large portions of the world into a crisis of epic proportions. It was also the time when the oil industry began to sound the alarm bells. In July 2005, Chevron unveiled an expensive ad campaign featuring a letter from CEO David O'Reilly, bluntly stating: "One thing is clear: the era of easy oil is over. [...] Demand is soaring like never before." This was the starkest admission from the oil industry that business isn't as usual, that "Big Oil" has turned into an oily version of Lewis Carroll's Red Queen – pumping faster and faster just to replace its reserves. (As it turns out for Mr. O'Reilly, business is as usual. After his retirement from Chevron he was appointed by Saudi King Abdullah in 2010 to be a member of Aramco's board of directors.) Other oil executives followed. In 2007, Christophe de Margerie, the boss of Total, declared that the world would not be able to increase its production beyond 100 million b/d, let alone 120 million b/d that would be needed by 2030. "We all think the same, it's just a question of whether we say it."[14]

All this led politicians to respond. In the January 2006 State of the Union Address then President George W. Bush uttered the famous line "America is addicted to oil, which is often imported from unstable parts of the world." Five months later, GM, which until then was flirting with futuristic and completely unrealistic hydrogen cars, unveiled the practical and exciting plug-in hybrid Chevy Volt.

Seven years later, America's vehicles are still, for the most part, dependent exclusively on petroleum products. But conceptually, the idea of fuel competition is no longer a lofty one. One of the leading voices representing this view is the United States Energy Security Council, a high level group of former cabinet secretaries and retired business and military leaders focused on the imperative of reducing the strategic importance of oil and on ubiquitous fuel competition as a means of doing so. The group, which includes former Secretary of State George Shultz, former Secretaries of Defense Harold Brown and William Perry, former Fed Chairman Alan Greenspan, former Governor of Pennsylvania Tom Ridge, former secretaries of the interior, transportation, agriculture, Navy and Air Force, three former national security advisors, retired senators, a former CIA director, a former president of Shell Oil Company, and a Nobel Laureate, has made significant strides in reshaping public understanding of the oil challenge. As two of the group's founding members opined in the *New York Times* Op-Ed page, "Competition is a bedrock of our American way of life. It's time to introduce it into our fuel market."[15] To learn more about the Council, which we are honored to advise, visit its website at www.usesc.org.

Much still needs to be done. As we saw, the early 20th century's shift from choice to petropoly lasted three decades. Do we have three decades to turn the wheel back? Having seen the consequences of dependence on what O'Reilly called "easy oil" we dread to think what dependence on "difficult oil" might look like. If we are to put an end to petropoly, we should strive in transportation for the scale of fuel diversity and continuous arbitrage opportunities our electricity grid provides.

Follow the grid

Interestingly, when it comes to electricity, America has done a fine job in achieving fuel diversification. In 1950, the United States consumed 370 gigawatt of electricity. Roughly half of it was generated from coal. The other half was provided by oil, natural gas and hydroelectric power. Over the next 20 years, electricity demand doubled, but the fuel mix remained the same. But by 1980, largely in response to the oil shocks of the 1970s and to maturing technology, a new source of power, nuclear, began to carve a growing niche in the nation's fuel mix, reaching 20 percent of power generation within 20 years. The nuclear sector grew primarily at the expense of volatile and costly petroleum based power generation. Hence, oil, which in 1977 accounted for 17 percent of America's electricity generation, has dropped to merely one percent today. In recent years, partly due to the concern about coal fueled emissions and partly due to cost improvements in wind and solar technologies, non-hydro renewable energy (primarily wind, solar and geothermal) has gained a growing albeit still small foothold in our electricity fuel mix accounting for nearly five percent of U.S. electrical generation in 2011. According to the Energy Information Administration (EIA), this share will increase to more than 12 percent in 2035. The evolution of America's electricity fuel mix has largely gone unnoticed by the end users. Our transmission lines, transformers, distributers, control systems all the way to our electrical appliances and light bulbs are agnostic as to how the electrons running through them are generated. No American has been forced to replace a coffee machine or a dishwasher because a public utility changed its fuel mix.

The comparison between the electricity and transportation sectors is instructive. While our electricity system has made giant strides toward fuel diversification, the transportation sector has remained virtually monopolized by oil. Today, barely five percent of our total transportation fuel comes from non-petroleum sources.

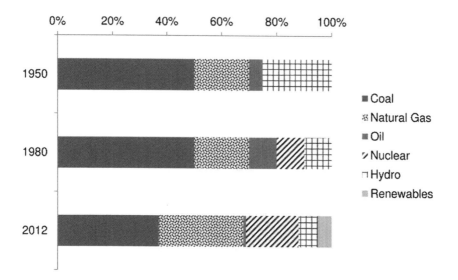

The diversification of America's electricity system 1950-2012

Fuel diversification is the most important prerequisite of achieving energy security. In a well-diversified electricity system disruption in supply or a price spike in one source of power can be compensated by a shift to another. This type of system in which fuels made from a variety of commodities – coal, natural gas, biomass, oil, etc. – compete against each other would greatly improve the economic outcome for consumers of transportation fuel. Just as the grid is agnostic as to what type of energy was used to make the electricity it transmits, our cars and trucks as well as our fuel distribution system and the rest of the infrastructure that handles fuels can be open to a diversified fuel mix. Several vehicle technologies enable drivers to enjoy fuel competition: flex fuel engines capable of working on any blend of gasoline and alcohol, compressed natural gas vehicles, different versions of battery powered vehicles, diesel engines that can run on both conventional and non-petroleum diesel, and perhaps in the future, if their economics improve, fuel cell vehicles. No doubt, over time more technologies will join the list. The questions of cost, of what – if any – is the role of government in enabling or speeding their proliferation, and of the barriers to market penetration such technologies face are all important and will be discussed in detail in the coming chapters. In the absence of fuel competition, most of the 13-16 million new vehicles that roll onto America's roads every year, each with a street life of about 15 years, will be unable to use anything but petroleum fuels. And that, with its attendant security and economic implications, would be a tragedy.

3
HOPE AND CHANGE: AMERICA'S NATURAL GAS

We are the Saudi Arabia of natural gas.
President Barack Obama
We are all losing our shirts today. {...} We're making no money.
It's all in the red.
Rex W. Tillerson, Chairman and CEO, Exxon Mobil Corporation[1]

A mere decade ago the United States faced a natural gas crisis. In testimony before the Congressional Joint Economic Committee in May of 2003, then Federal Reserve Chairman Alan Greenspan warned that tight natural gas supplies presented "an extremely serious problem" and noted "the inability of heightened gas well drilling to significantly augment" production.[2] Prices rose from less than $2 per million British Thermal Units (mmbtu) in 1999 to about $8 in August of 2005. It was about to get worse. Hurricane Katrina knocked out some Gulf Coast production capacity, and prices hit $12.

There is not one global market for natural gas as there is for oil. The price of natural gas varies across geographies. Transporting natural gas across non-contiguous territories requires either building a very long and expensive pipeline and signing contracts which serve to tie producers and consumers of the gas to each other over the long haul, or converting it at high pressure and low temperature into liquefied natural gas (LNG) whereupon it can be loaded on dedicated tankers and shipped overseas for purchase wherever regasification facilities exist. So while natural gas prices spiked in the United States to the highest levels in the industrial world, there were plenty of countries in which prices were quite low, and it is to those countries that much of the natural gas based chemical production formerly situated in the United States migrated as prices rose. In testimony submitted to the Environment and Public Works Committee in March 2004, the American Chemistry Council noted, "In the past five years, the U.S. chemical industry lost $50 billion to foreign competition." Then President of Bayer Corp. Attila Molnar put it bluntly: "It is a very, very serious issue," adding "You shift manufacturing or production [to] where you produced the cheapest. [...] Production in the U.S. is in danger today." Vice president for energy at Dow Chemical Co., which shuttered three U.S. plants between 2002 and 2004, pointed out "These jobs didn't leave the U.S. because of labor costs, they left the U.S. because of uncompetitive energy costs."[3] That was then, and this is now. Low gas prices are back, net natural gas imports are down to their lowest level since 1992, and the reason is a combination of technological innovation, persistence, and cooperative geology.

The frack factor

In the 1980s, a Texas petroleum engineer and independent energy producer George P. Mitchell pioneered a technology to extract natural gas from geological formations called shale. Gas shale is one of a number of unconventional sources of natural gas; others include coal bed methane which cohabits with coal deposits, tight sandstones, and methane hydrates – sponge like methane containing formations trapped under the seabed and which, to date, no one has figured out a way to extract commercially and safely. The shale is a porous geological sub stratum that varies in thickness from 50 to 500 feet and could extend horizontally for miles in depth from 1,500 to 6,500 feet. Those formations have been known for more than a century but they have not been of much value. The extraction process was just too expensive and technologically challenging. Against the skepticism of many of his industry colleagues, Mitchell continued to invest in the process until he was able to perfect the extraction method. What did the magic was the integration of two important technologies. The first, hydraulic fracturing, commonly known as fracking, is a complex process that involves drilling a wellbore into the dense shale rocks, then installing a cement casing into which perforation guns containing explosive charges are inserted to crack fissures in the shale at intervals of roughly 50-80 feet. At this stage, water mixed with sand and chemicals is pumped in at very high pressure. This fragments the rock, opening up tiny fissures through which the trapped gas can escape. The gas bubbles out and is captured in a well that brings it to the surface, where it can be piped off. But fracking alone was insufficient to bring shale gas to market in such large quantities. The real breakthrough was the combination of fracking with the second technology – horizontal drilling, a technology which Mitchell's partner, the independent Oklahoma City-based Devon Energy, perfected. In just about five years, improvement in horizontal drilling technology allowed drillers to expand the penetration of their horizontal pipes from a short 100 to 1,000 feet to a mindboggling 8,000-10,000 feet. Drilling horizontally allows us to frack rock volume an order of magnitude larger than would be the case with vertical drilling. "When you do a vertical drill you get just the depth of the shale formation. When you go horizontal you get the whole banana," explained John Hofmeister, former President of Shell Oil Company.[4]

As a result of Mitchell's doggedness and Devon's technical competence, shale gas became not just a commercial reality but a true game changer in America's energy landscape. Shale gas has earned itself a growing share of our domestic energy portfolio, and it has done so in an amazingly short time. As little as seven years ago, analysts and politicians believed that the United States could not drill its way out of a natural gas shortage. A June 2005 white paper by Senator James M. Inhofe, then Chairman of the Senate Committee on Environment and Public Works, noted "the days of low gas prices are over, and the nation is in the midst of a very real natural gas crisis."[5] At that time shale gas was only one percent of natural gas supply. Today, it makes one up third of America's gas output, and within two decades, assuming the economics pan out, it could reach 50 percent. The ramp up in exploration and production is impressive. In the Annual Energy Outlook 2010, technically recoverable shale gas resources were estimated to be 368 trillion cubic feet. A year later, the estimate shot up to 862 trillion cubic feet, a 134 percent increase in just one year. The U.S. Geological Survey estimated that the Marcellus Shale alone, a layer of rock that stretches across Pennsylvania and into New York and West Virginia, holds 84 trillion cubic feet of undiscovered gas that can be recovered with existing technology — more than Libya or Kuwait or 42 times the amount it estimated in 2002.[6] The U.S. Energy Information Administration's Annual Energy Outlook 2012 estimated that unlocking of the shale reserves brings total U.S. technically recoverable natural gas resources to 2,214 trillion cubic feet. Other estimates go as high as 2,629 trillion cubic feet.[7] This could have profound implications for energy security not only for the United States but also for the rest of the world. The International Energy Agency suggests that as a result of this development a "Golden Age of Gas" might be in the making.[8] Alan Greenspan described shale gas as an "extraordinary bonanza." John Rowe, the chief executive of Exelon, a utility company which derives almost all its power from nuclear power, says that shale gas is one of the most important energy revolutions of his lifetime.[9] *Time Magazine* commentator Fareed Zakaria framed it as "the biggest shift in energy in generations. And its consequences — economic and political — are profoundly beneficial to the United States."[10] The State

Department, which normally doesn't do the bidding of oil and gas interests, has begun promoting the technology abroad, saying that if it were
adopted in Eastern Europe, India and China, where the world's largest
economically recoverable shale deposit is located, it would reduce Russian
and Middle Eastern influence in those regions.[11]

Known and unknown unknowns

Yet, despite the talk about a "natural gas revolution" there are many
unanswered questions about shale gas. Just as the consensus a decade
ago about a looming North American natural gas shortage, a new high
price equilibrium, and a need for steadily increasing imports proved
itself wrong so could the projections of a natural gas glut. The shale gas
extraction process is extremely complex, and experience with the current
technology is limited to a few geological formations where the recovery
conditions are optimal. It is far less certain that those conditions are representative of the entire U.S. reserve base, not to mention those in China
and Europe. (In June 2012 Exxon announced it is pulling the plug on its
shale gas operation in Poland, Europe's most enthusiastic shale gas player,
after Poland's shale formation failed to deliver commercial quantities.)
We do not know the rate of depletion, the representative cost of recovery
and the full environmental implications of fracking. Could shale gas be
the energy industry's equivalent of a dot com bubble, as a controversial
New York Times article implied?[12]

As Donald Rumsfeld once said, there are known unknowns and
unknown unknowns. One of the known unknowns is how much of our
gas shale endowment is economically recoverable. After all, not all formations look like the Marcellus. Another known unknown is leakage.
Much of the public support for using natural gas among those concerned
about greenhouse gas emissions is the fact that generating a kilowatt-
hour's worth of electricity with a natural gas turbine emits about half as
much carbon dioxide as generating the same electricity at a coal plant.
However, some environmentalists are concerned that extracting natural
gas from the ground or the sea could release unburned methane which
is in orders of magnitude more potent a greenhouse gas than carbon
dioxide. From the environmentalist perspective, leaks of even 2.5 percent
would make natural gas a loser compared to coal. How much of the gas
leaks? No one knows for sure. From the industry's perspective, gas leaking into the air makes the wooshing sound of money going up in smoke.

As for the unknown unknowns, just like with other new technologies, unintended consequences take time to surface. One possible example: what would be the long term implications of a sustained underground bombing campaign followed by injection of millions of gallons of liquids on the geological makeup of the earth? Do the freak (and decidedly minor) earthquakes that have occurred recently in Virginia, Texas, and New York have anything to do with the fracking frenzy? For now, an unknown unknown.

The shale gas revolution has emerged so fast that science and policy are playing catch up and it will take years before many of the questions are satisfactorily answered. But despite the open questions, what we do know with a high level of certainty is that an enormous amount of natural gas is parked in our soil waiting for a market. It remains to be seen how much of it is recoverable at what price levels. Now that we know how to extract it and assuming we can do it safely, it is time to think about what it will take to enable arbitrage between oil and natural gas in the transportation fuel sector.

From Little Big Oil to Really Big Gas

In *Turning Oil into Salt,* we pointed out that the investor owned oil companies commonly referred to by various demagogues as "Big Oil" actually control a very small share of global oil reserves – less than eight percent. Fourteen of the world's top 20 oil and gas companies are government controlled National Oil Companies (NOCs). International Oil Companies (IOCs) like Exxon, Shell, BP and ChevronTexaco are ranked 12th, 13th, 16th and 19th respectively. The top 10 reserve holders are state monopolies such as Saudi Aramco, Russia's Gazprom, National Iranian Oil Company, PetroChina, and Petróleos de Venezuela, S.A (PDVSA). Saudi Aramco alone owns about three times more than the combined reserves of all the super majors. The real "Big Oil" is OPEC, with 78 percent of world oil reserves, and the other NOCs while the IOCs are actually Little Big Oil.

Whenever gasoline prices rise, populist politicians tend to point a blaming finger at Little Big Oil and refer to oil companies' profits as "obscene," calling for a heavy handed approach toward them. During the 2008 presidential campaign, when gasoline prices stood firmly above $4, then Senator Barack Obama called for taxing "windfall profits" that the industry was allegedly making. His rival for the Democratic nomination,

Senator Hillary Clinton, proclaimed to the sound of raucous cheers "I want to take those profits, and I want to put them into a strategic energy fund" to invest in new energy technologies.[13] Perhaps her audience didn't grasp that if you permit government to confiscate the profits of one particular industry and use them to fund its competitors you don't get to draw the line at just that industry.

Also, while oil company profits can be eye popping in absolute numbers, they are not that different from those of other industries on a percentage basis: Exxon's profit margins on a percentage basis are no more "obscene" than Microsoft's or Starbucks'. Pulling the rug out from under Little Big Oil will only strengthen our dependence on the real titans of the global oil industry, the much less savory state controlled NOCs whose behavior is far worse by any yardstick. Consider the differences. IOCs operate with Human Rights Watch over one shoulder, the Foreign Corrupt Practices Act over the other, and the Securities and Exchange Commission breathing down their necks. Perhaps as a result, most IOCs embrace what has become known as "corporate social responsibility" in the countries and communities in which they operate. They establish social development funds, respect local laws and human rights, submit quarterly reports to their shareholders, work to improve the lives of those directly impacted by their operations; they must adhere to strict Western anti-corruption laws (which makes them much less attractive as business partners to your run of the mill autocrat), and, by and large, they operate in an environmentally responsible manner. NOCs, on the other hand, are notorious for turning a blind eye to human rights abuses, corruption and environmental degradation in the countries in which they operate. They lack transparency and accountability and have no legal restraints on bribing local officials to get preferential treatment. Unlike the profit driven super majors who pump as much as they are able, the only restraining factor being restricted access to new fields, which happen to be found mainly in countries where the industry is nationalized, NOCs and their controlling governments collude regularly to manipulate oil prices by limiting production. There are even more important reasons for unease about the strengthening of the NOCs at the expense of the IOCs. A large portion of the net income of the IOCs is plowed back into the U.S. economy in the shape of taxes and dividends to shareholders. This cannot be said about the NOCs whose governments use their money to undermine America and its policies. Americans whose retirement accounts are invested in the S&P 500 Index directly benefit from the IOCs profits and rising share prices. If that profit were made by Saudi Aramco instead of Chevron it would further enrich the House of Saud, but how exactly would that serve the American family? The U.S. oil and gas industry is responsible for 7.5 percent of the nation's GDP and supports 9.2 million Americans. How many American jobs are supported by Saudi Aramco or Gazprom?

Now, with the rise of natural gas, there is even more reason populist politicians ought to reconsider their sentiment to America's oil patch, as from there of all places could potentially come the key to breaking out of Petropoly: Little Big Oil is well on its way to becoming Really Big Gas. With older oil fields producing less crude and newer ones either hard to reach or controlled by unfriendly nations, the major oil companies are increasingly betting their futures on natural gas. In the last five years, the portfolios of the five major oil companies have changed drastically, all reflecting a chase after natural gas investments. In 2005, ConocoPhilips made a $35 billion purchase of Burlington Resources, adding to its portfolio major gas assets in North America. In 2010, ExxonMobil made a huge bet on natural gas when it bought XTO Energy for $41 billion. It then acquired Denver-based Ellora Energy for $695 million, and spent another $575 million to purchase Petrohawk Energy's wells and reserves in Arkansas' Fayetteville Shale. Chevron purchased Atlas Corporation for $4.3 billion so it could get access to the gas shale deposits of the Appalachian region. In 2010, Shell brought East Resources, one of the largest independent gas companies in the Appalachian Basin, for $4.7 billion in cash, increasing Shell's total shale gas acreage in the United States to about 3.6 million acres. Shell president, Marvin Odum, announced that by 2012 his company will produce more gas than oil.[14] Non-American energy companies have also entered the shale play. French oil giant Total SA whose CEO Christophe de Margerie announced in the fall of 2007 that global oil production is peaking, spent $800 million in a joint venture with Chesapeake Energy, America's second-largest gas producer. The deal gave Total access to 25 percent of Chesapeake's Barnett Shale assets. BP and the Norwegian Statoil have also entered joint ventures with Chesapeake, purchasing assets in the Fayettville and the Marcellus.

The rapid expansion of America's domestic gas industry has created an unforeseen challenge for the producers: supply has expanded much faster than demand and has thus brought to a collapse of gas prices below the point where much of the recently expanded capacity is profitable. Historically, natural gas prices have always tracked oil prices, but as the graph below shows, the shale revolution has disconnected prices of the two commodities. Since the onset of the Great Recession, oil prices, as well as the price of all other commodities, have rebounded more or less to their pre-2009 level, whereas gas prices continue to decline. The price of natural gas dropped by about 80 percent between 2008 and 2012. The result: we are awash with cheap – dirt cheap – natural gas, but the commodity's traditional users, utilities and chemical producers are not yet able to absorb much of it. As Aubrey McClendon, former chief executive of Chesapeake Energy, put it "natural gas is not oversupplied in the United States; it is under-demanded."[15]

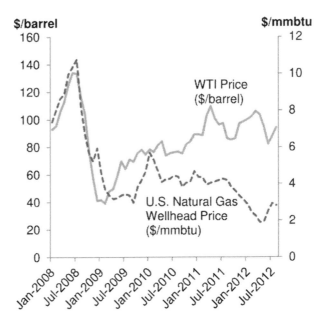

The divorce of oil and natural gas prices

If demand remains stagnant and natural gas prices remain low, the industry will have little incentive to invest in further growth, and the economic benefits associated with the industry, including the creation of approximately 870,000 jobs and the potential addition of $118 billion to economic growth by 2015, will be erased.[16] Opening vehicles to fuels made from natural gas and allowing this resource to compete against oil will drive a demand surge that will send prices to a more economically sustainable price level for producers, giving the industry a sufficiently profitable horizon to continue and grow this sector, to the benefit of our economy.

The departure of the oil majors from their traditional business model, as they venture into the unconventional natural gas universe is a seminal development. In the past, Little Big Oil viewed fuel competitors to gasoline as unwanted competition: every gallon of non-petroleum fuel sold meant less demand for gasoline – a zero sum game. Today, Little Big Oil's downstream operations, which process crude into petroleum products such as gasoline and diesel, are reporting a significant drop in gains due to lower demand.[17] For these reasons and others, we foresee a growing interest within the industry for natural gas-derived fuels at the pump coexisting with gasoline. More demand for natural gas means higher prices which in turn means faster return on investment on the shale projects and increased appetite for additional investment. This means more investment, more tax revenues, better dividends in our pension funds and investment portfolios, and more jobs. In other words, Little Big Oil might just hold the key to transforming the transportation fuel market.

Export or keep?

But what if the natural gas producers decided to take the trillions of cubic feet of unwanted gas, cool them to a temperature of -260 degrees Fahrenheit to convert them into LNG, and send them overseas instead of selling them at home? A tanker can carry 600 times more natural gas as LNG than in gaseous form. It is a good way to deliver natural gas to stranded markets in which the commodity is not available and cannot be served by pipelines. LNG accounts today for roughly 10 percent of the world's natural gas demand. In order for two countries to engage in LNG trade, three components must be in place: a liquefaction plant on the exporting side, a regasification terminal where the LNG is allowed to expand and reconvert into gas on the receiving end and a double hulled LNG tanker which shuttles back and forth. Since the United States has been primarily a net natural gas importer, it has 12 operational receiving terminals but no liquefaction plants, which are much more expensive to build. Building a liquefaction terminal is a grueling process. Environmentalists and NIMBYists can make permitting and siting of LNG terminals almost as nightmarish as building a nuclear power plant. Manufacturers, utilities and consumer advocates, concerned that exporting natural gas will drive up electricity prices and discourage investment in domestic manufacturing, are pushing for legislation to restrict exports. But despite the bureaucratic hurdles and the high capital investment, on its face the economics of LNG are too attractive to ignore. A thousand cubic feet of gas currently trades in the United States for under $3. The all-in processing and shipping cost for LNG is about $4, so that equates to $7 natural gas when delivered overseas. The same amount of gas sells for $8 to $9 in Europe and could reach as much as $16 to $19 in Asia. One could think of several European countries that would be happy to reduce their dependence on Russian gas by switching to American LNG even if that means paying a premium. Japan, which post-Fukushima is distancing itself from nuclear power, will need vast quantities of imported gas. So will China and India. With such potential market over the horizon, LNG advocates believe that once the capital investment is recovered and even with the extra expense for liquefaction, transport and regasification, there can be nice room for trans-oceanic arbitrage.

Perhaps, but just for a short while. Suppose American companies decide to sell LNG to Japan. Assume the Japanese purchaser is willing to pay $19 per mmbtu, and a 10-year contract is signed. The laws of economics argue that from the moment the first gas shipment reaches Japan's shores the spread between the United States' and Japan's gas prices begins to shrink rapidly. Here is why: Once gas is exported from the U.S., local excess supply falls and thus the domestic price of gas begins to rise. At the same time, once Japan's market is better supplied its price begins to fall. But this is not all. Other gas-rich countries might, too, build LNG terminals, and due to their advantageous geographical location might offer the Japanese better terms, posing serious competition to the American LNG. What is likely to happen should the United States become a major LNG exporter is that first, we'll move into a more unified global market for natural gas, as we have now for oil, and second the other gas giants – Russia, Iran, Qatar, Saudi Arabia and the United Arab Emirates – will have every incentive to form an OPEC-like natural-gas cartel to restrict supply to the market and counterbalance the United States. The aforementioned five countries have already been engaged steadily and stealthily in discussions on the establishment of such a cartel. That will drive natural gas prices up higher in the U.S. than they would have gone otherwise, and while it will certainly benefit those who own and sell the gas, overall through higher electricity and chemical prices it would be a drain on the economy. As long as LNG plays a small part in international natural gas trading, it is not likely to be cartelized, but the more fungible the commodity becomes, the more likely it is to follow in oil's footsteps.

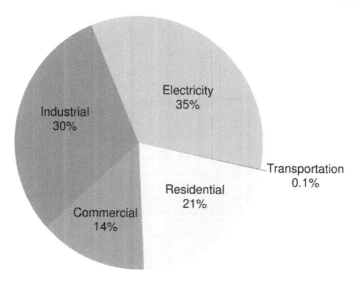

Natural gas end use markets

All of the above points are commercial considerations each company has to assess. Before rushing to export our gas bonanza, investors ought to compare the economics of this option with those of keeping the gas at home to make fuels that compete with those made from oil. A barrel of oil contains about the same amount of energy as 5,600 cubic feet of natural gas. This means that if oil and gas had an equal value, at $100/barrel oil, the price of 1,000 cubic feet of natural gas would have to be roughly $18. But as mentioned, it is far lower than that, less than $3. If a barrel of oil was selling for the same amount of money per unit energy as natural gas, it would cost us $16. Put it differently, per unit of energy, oil costs five times as much as gas. Let's take a second look at the LNG option in light of these numbers. Choosing the export option essentially means that we import $100 worth oil while exporting $16 worth of oil equivalent natural gas. This means $84 in trade deficit for every barrel of oil imported rather than replaced with gas.

To be sure, using natural gas to make transportation fuels will increase demand for gas and thus its cost. But here's the key: as the capacity for making natural gas-based fuels grows and supply increases to the point that the two commodities are in a head to head competition over the fuel market, this competition will serve to drag down the price of oil even as it drags up the price of gas. Competition that drags oil price down to say $45 a barrel and natural gas price up to $7 per mmbtu will have a profound impact on our trade deficit, and while it wouldn't be that great for those who spin dreams about oil shale,[18] it would be a huge boon for the natural gas industry, stimulating domestic investments and along the way, driving domestic job creation. The industry and the economy writ large would be missing a huge opportunity if the focus on exporting blinds us to other options and if we don't open the door to natural gas based fuels. Currently, natural gas is used roughly equally among three sectors: power generation, industry and residential/commercial uses. Less than one percent of our natural gas supply is used as automotive fuel, and while in the past 20 years natural gas end use in electricity generation has almost quadrupled, there has been almost no growth in its use in the transportation sector since the 1970s.[19] Chronically high oil prices coupled with historically low natural gas prices present a solid case for changing that. Let's examine how to do it best.

4
THE TIME FACTOR

I feel the need, the need for speed.

Maverick in Top Gun

*To search for perfection is all very well, but to look
for heaven is to live here in hell.*

Sting

There's nothing quite like hitting the accelerator on a Tesla Roadster from a full stop. There's no waiting for fuel to make its way through the fuel line to the engine and the thrill of the car's leap forward is addictive. It is the perfect car for people who love to drive, have sufficiently fast reflexes to appreciate what it can do, and sufficiently deep pockets to buy it. Founded in 2003, the Silicon Valley-based space entrepreneur Elon Musk came up with a unique business model in Tesla Motors. It catered to affluent, cost insensitive early adopters, offering the Roadster, a limited series of 2,400 electric luxury sports cars with a range greater than 200 miles per charge. Beginning its journey with a high-end car, Tesla accomplished two important goals. First, it proved that electric vehicle performance is not inferior in any way to that of an equivalent internal combustion engine powered high-end sports car. Anyone who has test driven a Roadster would attest to that. Second, selling cars in the range of $100,000-$140,000 a piece enabled the company to accumulate the cash necessary to take it to the next phase – the company's subsequent car, the Model S sedan, which started selling in 2012 for roughly half the price of the Roadster. This trickle down strategy aims to give rise to the company's next model of electric vehicle, the Model X electric crossover SUV and, as of 2015, the even more affordable $30,000 Bluestar. Tesla's bold strategy inspired the Big Three automakers to accelerate the development of their own electric vehicles (EV) programs. Former General Motors' Vice Chairman Robert Lutz recalled how Tesla was the fly that finally caused the Big Three to sneeze: "All the geniuses here at General Motors kept saying lithium-ion technology is 10 years away, and Toyota agreed with us – and boom, along comes Tesla. So I said, 'How come some tiny little California startup, run by guys who know nothing about the car business, can do this, and we can't?' That was the crowbar that helped break up the log jam."[1]

Indeed, visiting any of the international auto shows from Paris to Detroit, one might get the impression that the auto industry is going electric in a big way. General Motors (GM), Nissan, Ford, Toyota and Chrysler have all rolled out new designs of electric vehicles and plug-in hybrid electric vehicles (PHEV). Pure electric vehicles run only on the power stored in the battery — no liquid fuel tank - and their range is limited by the battery's storage capacity, while PHEVs have both a battery and a liquid fuel engine so there is no compromise on range. In 2010, GM began marketing the Chevrolet Volt plug-in hybrid which has an all-electric range of 35-40 miles as well as a liquid fuel tank, and Nissan came out with the 100-mile range all-electric Leaf. In 2012, new models appeared in showrooms including the Ford Focus and Honda Fit, both with a battery range of 100 miles, and the 15-mile electric range Toyota Prius Plug-in Hybrid. The electric vehicle boom has opened the door to a new breed of small and innovative automakers specializing on various niche markets: high end sports cars, vans, pickup trucks, etc. Fisker, Coda Automotive, the Chinese BYD and, of course, Tesla are all on the path to assuming a foothold in the global auto market.

Tesla Model S followed by the Roadster.
Courtesy: Tesla Motors

The electric vehicle is not just a battery mounted on wheels. It has the potential to be an innovation platform, "an iPhone on steroids," as

New York Times columnist Thomas Friedman noted.[2] Hardly a day goes by without an announcement on new breakthroughs in battery technology, recharging infrastructure or demand management technologies for electric vehicles and other accessories and peripheral services. As lithium-ion battery technology surpasses the currently dominant rechargeable battery technologies, lead acid and nickel metal hydride, the global automotive battery market is projected to grow fivefold in the coming decade with revenues expected to reach $54 billion by 2020.[3] Demand for charging stations and other peripherals for electric vehicles will quintuple in the coming decade to reach over $20 billion. Investors too have taken notice, and electric cars were hailed as one of the top five investment trends for 2011.[4]

The prospect of electrifying transportation is compelling and exciting. From a strategic perspective, the most important upside of electrified transportation is the fact that 99 percent of U.S. electricity is generated from non-petroleum energy sources like coal, natural gas, nuclear power and renewable energy like hydro, geothermal, solar and wind. So vehicles that can be plugged in and run at least partially on grid electricity put all of those energy sources squarely in competition with oil. One way to take advantage of natural gas' low cost is to use it to generate electricity which among other things can be used to charge electrified vehicles. However, because fueling with electricity is so much less expensive than fueling with gasoline, even with the current electricity generation mix, this is almost like gilding the lily – it won't make a huge difference to the cost of electric miles from a consumer perspective. From an economic standpoint, fueling with electrons is less costly than fueling with practically any liquid fuel (no, we aren't ignoring the battery cost, we'll get to that later.) The cost of travelling a mile on $4 a gallon gasoline is roughly 14 cents. Running a car for the same mile on electricity would cost far less. The national average price of residential electricity in early 2012 was 11.5 cents per kilowatt-hour. States like Utah, Idaho or Indiana enjoy electricity prices as low as 7-9 cents while in California and New York the price is 15-17 cents. Most electric cars drive two to four miles per kilowatt-hour which means a cost of mile driven is a real bargain: usually under 4 cents, and in the worst case scenario about 8.5 cents. Electricity is not only a cheap fuel, it is also, relatively speaking, clean. Even if the electricity is generated from coal, driving a mile on electricity is cleaner than on petroleum fuel: the big power plants generating electricity for utilities are inherently more efficient than the little ones that power our cars. Mass proliferation of electrified vehicles would also improve the efficiency of the grid. The big, base load, 24/7 power plants that provide the back-bone of our power supply aren't powered down during those parts of the day when usage is at low — the excess energy they generate during those hours is wasted: grounded or dissipated as heat. But low demand times – like nighttime – are precisely the times when most parked cars would be charged, storing in batteries (and paying for) all of the energy that is currently a dead weight loss to utilities. According to the Department of Energy's Pacific Northwest National Laboratory report, the current grids' reserve capacity would suffice to power up to 84 percent of U.S. cars and trucks assuming power is drawn during off-peak hours.[5] An additional study by the North American Electric Reliability Corporation (NERC) shows that a 25 percent penetration of electric vehicles in any given area in the year 2030 would require less than a 5.5 percent increase in genera-tion.[6] So if there are hurdles to the electrification of transportation, power availability isn't one of them.

Quite the opposite actually: electrified vehicles can be especially use-ful when power is not available. The derecho storms of the summer of 2012 and the week long blackouts inflicted in their wake were the red alert to those living in the Washington, DC metro area that there is much to be done to upgrade and secure the American power grid. Frustrated by repeated outages, some people are buying expensive generators, but for PHEV or EV owners there is an easier option: buying inexpensive invert-ers which convert the DC power from their car battery to the AC power needed to run their sump pump, refrigerator and other critical appli-ances. In the case of a pure electric vehicle, once the battery is drained so is your blackout power supply, whereas with a PHEV, your backup power will last as long as you have a supply of liquid fuel. Toyota and Nissan have announced vehicle-to-home bi-directional charging systems which accomplish pretty much the same thing albeit at significantly higher cost.

The revenge of the electric car?

All of this explains why so much has been done in recent years to advance the electrification of the transportation sector with a primary focus on cars and light trucks (it's worth noting that vehicle electrification has advanced in leaps and bounds in China not in the automotive sector but rather for electric mopeds and e-bikes, and millions have chosen to pur-chase electrics instead of riding atop smelly and loud two stroke engines, which in some cities have been outlawed for air quality reasons. There are over one hundred and twenty million e-bikes in China.) Congress has provided a policy framework in support of electrification. The Energy Independence and Security Act of 2007 provided important provisions for battery operated vehicles. The Emergency Economic Stabilization Act of 2008 (aka the bailout) provided tax credits of up to $7,500 per car to early adopters. The American Recovery and Reinvestment Act of 2009 (aka the stimulus) allocated $2.4 billion in loans to three electric vehicle factories in Tennessee, Delaware, and California and an additional $2 billion in grants to support 30 factories that produce batteries, motors, and other EV components. Additional funds were committed to various transportation electrification demonstration and deployment projects. Other electrification bills are pending before Congress. In his 2011 State of the Union address, President Obama called for putting one million electric vehicles on the road by 2015, affirming and highlighting the aim of building American leadership in technologies that reduce the dependence on oil.[7] The recent increases in CAFE standards, requiring vehicle manufacturers to increase fuel economy through 2025, are also likely to encourage the expanded market entry of electric drive technologies.

In light of the frenzy of activity no wonder so many consider electricity the fuel of the future. While the progress made is impressive, some perspective is needed. As should be quite clear by now, we are big fans of vehicle electrification. Indeed, the Set America Free Coalition which we co-founded in 2004, in collaboration with the staunch electrified transportation advocates and trailblazers at our Coalition partner the California Cars Initiative (CalCars), was the first to bring plug-in hybrids (two 100+mpg converted Priuses) to Capitol Hill in 2006, when Washington DC's flavor of the month was hydrogen. The Senators and Representatives test driving those cars realized the technology is real and compelling even as the CEOs of the Big Three automakers proclaimed at a press conference nearby that electrification was not on their agenda. So we write the following with the firm conviction that vehicle electrification would have tremendous benefits for our economy and security and should be pursued with all vigor: It is profoundly wrong to treat vehicle electrification as a silver bullet to the exclusion of solutions that could impact the near and mid-term and expect everything will be just peachy as the world makes its long and meandering way down the road to an electric Valhalla.

Unfortunately, it is going to take a very long time to get to a point where a large portion of the U.S. vehicle fleet is fully or partially electric. In 2010, the number of cars worldwide surpassed one billion.[8] The market for all-electric and plug-in hybrid electric cars in the United States is tiny, amounting to fewer than 20,000 sales in 2011 out of total light-vehicle sales of 12.8 million. This means that only one in 640 new vehicles was electric. China's government plan to advance the sale of 500,000 plug-in vehicles by 2015 and five million by 2020 is also falling short of expectations. Only 8,000 cars were sold in 2011, almost all of them bought by government fleets. Total global sales for plug-in hybrid and electric vehicles in 2011 amounted to about 43,000 cars, according to Bloomberg New Energy Finance. Those numbers will surely rise in the coming years but by how much and by when? Numerous analyses have been conducted trying to project plug-in vehicle market penetration; each had its own assumptions about the pace of cost reduction, consumer acceptance and oil prices. But as Table 4.1 shows the aggregate of the key studies is sobering. Most forecasts show that plug-in vehicles will account for no more than 5-10 percent of the global market for new vehicles by 2020. In July 2011, the International Energy Agency reported that the major automakers themselves project 1.4 million plug-in vehicles will be sold in 2020 – a mere 2 percent of new vehicle sales.[9]

Table 4.1: Projections for plug-in vehicle market penetration[10]

Study	Projection
U.S. National Academy of Sciences (2010)	3% of sales by 2015 and 15% by 2035
Credit Suisse (2009)	7.9% of sales by 2030
US Energy Information Administration (2011)	1.8% of sales in 2020 and 3.8% by 2035
IHS Global Insight (2010)	20% of sales in 2030
Roland Berger Strategy Consultants (2012)	2.2%-8.2% of sales by 2020
The Boston Consulting Group, (2010)	5% of sales by 2020
Deloitte, (2010)	3.1% of sales by 2020

Important as sales figures are, the real question to ask is at what point will plug-in vehicles make a substantial share - say one third - of our surface fleet? Consider the case of hybrid vehicles, which began to appear in the U.S. market in 1999 when Toyota released the Prius, the first hybrid four-door sedan. The car was a smashing success. Tree huggers bought it for environmental reasons; security hawks bought it to drive OPEC out of business, techies loved the innovation and slick look and busy motorists took advantage of the HOV lane permits some states granted. But despite the enthusiastic acceptance, the consumer tax incentives, the large scale purchase by federal, state and municipal governments, the enactment of increases in required average fuel economy which drove automakers to produce more hybrids and the spike in gasoline prices which improved the appeal of the technology to consumers, by May 2011, twelve years after the commercialization of the technology, hybrids represented 2.4 percent of total new vehicle sales, down from a peak of 2.9 percent in 2008.[11] This means that a cumulative total of only two million hybrids were sold in the United States – barely one percent of the overall U.S. fleet. Globally, hybrids are projected to make up roughly seven percent of vehicle sales by 2020, a figure that will capture one half of one percent of the global fleet of one billion vehicles.[12] Will plug-in hybrids or pure electric vehicles, a more expensive and, in the case of the former, slightly more complex technology, fare much better?

Suppose the Obama administration succeeds in its goal to facilitate the commercialization of one million plug-in vehicles by 2015. At that point the U.S. fleet of passenger vehicles and light trucks will stand at 255 million. This means that plug-in vehicles will make up 0.5 percent of the fleet. How many years will it take for them to comprise one third of the fleet? Here too, some assumptions should be made. We decided to take the optimist's outlook, assuming that plug-in vehicles will make five percent of new vehicle sales by 2020 and 20 percent by 2030. Based on our assumptions, as Table 4.2 shows, plug-in vehicles will capture a significant portion of the automobile fleet only around 2040. A projection by the U.S. Energy Information Administration (EIA) shows lower penetration.[13]

Table 4.2: Projected rate of penetration for Plug-in Vehicles

Year	Cumulative number of PIV	Percentage of total US fleet
2015	1,000,000	0.5%
2020	4,000,000	1.5%
2025	9,100,000	3.2%
2030	22,000,000	7.5%
2035	51,000,000	16%
2040	103,000,000	32%

The sobering bottom line is this: given a 15 year vehicle turnover cycle and considering the likelihood of economically devastating oil shocks in the interim decades, vehicle electrification, important as it is, cannot prudently be viewed as the be-all-end-all solution but must be seen as complementary to other technologies. The problem is that in many quarters electrification is perceived as a panacea, and some electric vehicle advocates view other fuels or vehicle technologies as unnecessary distractions that delay the introduction of electric cars. Many in Washington have adopted this worldview. "Why bother opening cars to liquid fuel competition when electric cars are at the gate?" is a utopianist question we have heard too many times from members of Congress and their staff (the flavor of the month has switched to Compressed Natural Gas (CNG) vehicles for some politicians, but that's a story for another chapter.)

No doubt electrification is a necessary component to stripping oil of its strategic status and it looks increasingly likely that by the middle of the 21st century the electric motor could be the primary mode of propulsion in surface transportation. Yet, betting the farm on electrification to the exclusion of other solutions is a risky strategy that fails to account for the many years it will take the technology to capture a large enough swath of our auto market and for the risks to the United States economy in the absence of a fuel market that is open to viable near term competitors to oil based fuels in the interim period. It also fails to account for the fact that the shift to electrification will happen faster if we are wealthier as a nation. High oil prices sap our wealth. If we don't exert negative pressure on oil price in the near and mid-term by placing it in competition with other energy commodities, the hit our economy will continue to take will make it much harder for drivers to upgrade their vehicles to a new and better technology.

The time factor is not unique to electrified vehicles. The shift from early adopters to mass market purchases to broad based market penetration is a process every new technology goes through and for expensive durable goods it takes a long time. It took 26 years from the invention of black and white TV until the adoption of the technology by a quarter of the American population. It took 18 years for color TV to proliferate. The situation with other appliances is similar: radio took 31 years to penetrate, telephone 35, mobile phones 13, and computers 16. Any expectation that electric vehicles could somehow show a faster pace of penetration is unrealistic. After our home, the automobile is the average family's most expensive belonging. Its turnover is relatively slow, and it requires a broad array of supporting services related to maintenance, refueling and recycling.

Barriers to EV penetration

In *Turning Oil into Salt* we urged a focus on the "good enough" when it comes to batteries and electrified vehicles. In this as in other cases, the perfect is the enemy of the good. Good enough means a smaller battery, backup fuel tank, charge at home in a standard 220 outlet, no waiting for an expensive infrastructure roll-out. Based on the lessons learned from the stillborn push for electric vehicles in the 1990s, this time around the utility industry and many vehicle electrification advocates also initially focused on plug-in hybrid electrics as mass market end runs around anticipated hurdles.

When it comes to plug-in vehicles there are two main barriers to mass market adoption: range and cost. Limited range indeed poses a consumer acceptance problem for pure electrics. No one wants to be stuck in the middle of a highway looking for a plug or waiting six to eight hours at a rest station for the car battery to recharge. It's called range anxiety. Despite the fact that half of the cars on America's roads are driven 25 miles per day or less while most pure electric vehicles offer a range of 80-100 miles this anxiety is real. The range currently offered may cover the daily needs of a significant population of car owners; however this may not be enough to convince someone whose commuting distance is only 20 miles per day but whose mother lives in a nursing home 50 miles away to go electric. Lucy visits her mom only once a fortnight, typically in the evenings, but that trip is enough to dissuade her from abandoning her gasoline car. With an aging mother and the shaky economy, Lucy has enough stress in her life. The last thing she wants to worry about when visiting her mom is whether she'll make it back home. There are possible solutions for Lucy's trepidation. If Lucy's household is one of the millions of households owning two cars or more, she could use one of the conventional cars in those times she goes on longer trips and for the rest of the time drive on electricity for short haul commuting. If she lives in one of the countries where a company called Better Place is deploying pop-in, pop-out battery switching stations perhaps that might appeal to her. But for those looking for a car that does it all, doesn't require mass investments in infrastructure, and provides essentially the same experience as a "regular" car, plug-in hybrid electric vehicles shine. A PHEV would give Lucy all the range she needs as her liquid fuel engine kicks in when the battery runs out of power, and with a smaller and thus less expensive battery than a pure electric vehicle.

Which brings us to the more serious barrier – cost. Yes, fueling with electricity is much cheaper than fueling with gasoline. But the vehicle itself is more expensive. The Volt's 16kWh battery pack today costs more than $8,000. The Nissan Leaf's 24kWh battery with an average range of 80-100 miles costs around $12,000.[14] This makes an electric vehicle significantly more expensive than a comparable conventional gasoline powered vehicle. While much, if not all, of the initial investment is recouped over the lifetime of the car through lower fuel and maintenance costs, Americans are not known to make purchasing decisions based on net present value considerations, especially because most people don't keep a new car very long before replacing it. The price at the showroom must come down. While the industry is working hard to reduce the cost, it is not clear how fast the comparative costs can change over the next twenty years. In fact, even as production costs decline, it is quite likely that the price of plug-in vehicles to purchasers will actually go up before coming down. How come? Today, electric car buyers enjoy a tax credit of up to $7,500. The Nissan Leaf's 2011 sticker price is $32,780, but the $7,500 tax credit brings that down to a more reasonable sticker price of $25,280. Outside of the United States battery powered vehicles are also heavily supported by subsidies. In China, an E6 all-electric BYD with a range of 188 miles per charge sells at a sticker price of 369,800 yuan ($58,200). However, buyers in cities like Shenzhen could qualify for as much as 120,000 yuan ($18,878) in subsidies according to the National Development and Reform Commission's Shenzhen branch. In the UK, the Plug-in Car Grant started in January 2011 provides a 25 percent grant towards the cost of new plug-in cars capped at GB£5,000 ($7,800).

But how long will those subsidies remain in place? Will the price come down soon enough before political and fiscal pressure to phase out the subsidies mounts? Not likely. Under current U.S. law, the tax credit is bound to phase out once a qualified automaker sells 200,000 vehicles. This means that several years from now, consumers will no longer be eligible for a tax credit if they bought plug-in vehicles from GM and Nissan as those two companies will have probably reached the 200,000 car benchmark. The Chinese government announced that the amount of the subsidy will be reduced once 50,000 units are sold.[15] By 2020 almost every automaker will have exhausted its tax incentives quota. Unless Washington extends those tax incentives beyond the current 200,000-unit benchmark, something that seems increasingly unlikely under the current fiscal and political conditions, any price cutting due to mass production will be offset by a diminishing tax credit. Unless Moore's Law kicks in.

Is there a Moore's Law for batteries?

Since the bursting of the Dot Com bubble, a group of software entrepreneurs and investors have found the clean-tech sector and in particular the effort to wean America from oil to be the greenest pasture of all. Famed software luminaries like co-founder of Sun Microsystems Vinod Khosla who made significant investment in various biofuels ventures, Google co-founders Larry Page and Sergei Brin who declared war on fossil fuels writ large as well as invested in the adoption of electric vehicles, former Intel President Andy Grove who became a passionate advocate of electrification, Paypal co-founder and now the man behind Tesla, Elon Musk, former SAP executive who became founder and CEO of Better Place, Shai Agassi, and John Doerr, a notable venture capitalist at Kleiner Perkins Caufield & Byers have all found in the energy sector what they needed: an opportunity to change the world in a big way. There are many more: 3Com founder Robert Metcalfe, Hotmail investor Steve Jurvetson, eBay executive Steve Westly and the list goes on and on. The shift of so many visionary, highly entrepreneurial and well capitalized individuals from infotech to the vehicle and energy sector has done a lot of good for the fuel choice movement. The software magnates surely know how to build companies, how to enthuse investors and how to infect politicians with their vision. They detest what they consider the stolid dinosaurs of the oil and automobile industries; they view a car as a computer on wheels rather than a complex mechanical device, and hence they believe the solution to the world's energy challenge will come from the innovation hubs of Silicon Valley, not whatever remains of Detroit.

But applying the lessons those erstwhile info-techies have learned in the software industry which they fully understand to the automotive industry which they *think* they understand could be tricky. Better Place founder Shai Agassi, for example, wanted to emulate the cell phone model offering his audience (and potential customers) a vehicle miles subscription plan similar to that cell phone providers offer. You sign up for a certain number of electric miles per month and for a fixed fee you get a "complete commute solution."[16] Sounds simple and logical. The problem is that a car is not a cell phone, and a business model that works well in one market may not be applicable to another. Economics matter. This is why Agassi, who in 2007 promised: "If you go for four years, we'll subsidize your car or your fuel, and if you go for six years, we'll give you a free car" ended up doing neither when the cars finally became available for sale.[17] In his first commercial markets in Israel and Denmark, where gasoline prices are among the highest in the world and where both governments provided unprecedented tax incentives, there were no free cars. To the contrary, the price of the Renault Fluence, the only car Better Place actually sells, is higher than that of the gasoline-powered version. In October 2012, Agassi was removed from his CEO position and the company is fighting for its life.

The same type of erroneous analogy is commonly committed in what has come to be known as the Moore's Law of batteries. In 1965, Intel co-founder Gordon Moore famously predicted that the number of transistors on a chip would double roughly every two years, allowing the computing industry to grow at an accelerated pace. Moore was proved right when it came to semiconductors. The transistor count of the 1971 Intel 4004 was 2,300. Twenty years later, the Pentium had 3,100,000 and in 2011, the latest microprocessor had a transistor count of 2,600,000,000. This exponential improvement enabled semiconductors to be cheap and powerful enough to be embedded into all the platforms that support our increasingly internet-based society. Now techno-optimists argue that Moore's Law is also applicable to batteries (the theory is also frequently used to hype other forms of renewable energy technologies like solar power) predicting a similar exponential improvement curve for automotive batteries both in terms of cost and density. Shai Agassi projected in 2010 that "the cost per mile of the electric car battery will be cut in half every 18 months."[18] This is where he and his fellow tech wizards may be over-analogizing the universe from which they came. Battery innovation is dissimilar to microchips, and there are deep physical limits to battery improvement. Hype and sloganeering cannot change this fact. Here is why.

Battery prices will decline, surely but slowly

The value chain of the automotive battery for an electric car consists of eight steps: materials processing, manufacturing of cell components (anode, cathode, separator and electrolyte), cell assembly, modules creation, integration of the modules with a control system, the integration of the automotive battery in the car, the use of the battery throughout the lifetime of the vehicle and the battery's end of life – disposal and recycling. In order to assess the pace of battery cost reduction, each one of the steps should be analyzed, taking into consideration technological breakthroughs, value chain developments, government policies and exogenous factors like the price of oil and the overall economic conditions. In all eight steps one can see progress which could translate into some cost reduction. But in the end there is no secret about what it will take to reduce battery costs to consumers: higher production volumes, new technologies that will increase battery power densities, and perhaps new ownership models for batteries like the one Better Place offers, allowing consumers to capture and maximize the benefits of electrification without bearing the financial risk of owning a $10,000 box full of lithium and nickel. On all three fronts one can see noteworthy improvement. Energy density of the battery shows a 10-15 percent improvement every year and has been like that more or less for many years. The longevity of the battery shows a similar 10-15 percent improvement every year. But none of this comes close to the scale of Moore's Law. In other words, no quantum leaps appear to be in the cards.

Take the first step, the cost of raw materials, for example. A battery is a box full of commodities. Lithium, cobalt, nickel, graphite and rare earth elements make the anode, cathode, separator and electrolyte the primary component of each of the cells from which a battery is made. Altogether raw materials and processing make about 58 percent of the cost of a cell, the battery's building block.[19] These materials need to be mined in large quantities to meet the requirements of the automotive industry. That is not to say that there is a physical limitation on material availability. There isn't. The earth's crust is rich in minerals. While all told raw materials account for a big chunk of the battery cost, there are lots of different materials used in a battery, and each particular commodity accounts for a fairly small portion of the overall cost. Increases in the cost of a particular commodity would not have a profound impact on the total cost of the battery. So some sort of inherent material shortage is not an issue. But the stability of the battery supply chain depends on our ability to mine sufficient quantities of materials in relatively short time. That takes ramp up. The mining industry is doing its share, and scores of new mines for battery elements are being developed around the world. But the process of setting up a mine is lengthy and expensive. Permitting, engineering, and metallurgical and environmental testing take roughly 10 years to complete. In order for Moore's Law to take hold, our battery supply chain for the coming decades should have already been in place. It isn't. The price of raw materials is projected to go down by merely 10 percent by 2015, mainly driven by a decrease in the cost of cathode materials like nickel and cobalt. In the long term one can expect a 40 percent reduction.[20] So if you want to find a Moore's Law-type improvement for batteries, "you've got to go to an asteroid and come back with some new materials," as one battery company executive put it.[21]

The situation is not different in the other stages of battery production. The cost of a battery pack which includes the costs of the battery cells, the battery management system, and the packaging is currently $550/kWh, and expected to decline in the next few years to $390/kWh and in the long run below $265/kWh.[22] McKinsey expects battery pack prices to drop to $200/kWh by 2020 while Bloomberg New Energy Finance projects $150/kWh by 2030.[23] While that sounds promising, Bloomberg adds the caveat that the recent price drops are due primarily to massive over capacity in battery manufacturing – at a factor of almost ten – rather than to increases in cell manufacturing and battery assembly efficiency. In other words, what's driving down battery costs is unmet demand expectation for plug-in vehicles rather than breakthroughs in battery technology. Regardless of the reason, the projected cost reduction is encouraging but certainly not eye popping. At $200/kWh, a 24kWh battery pack like that of the Leaf would sell for roughly $4,800. A smaller plug-in hybrid battery pack would be less costly. One reason for our skepticism about Moore's Law in batteries is the overall lack of competitiveness in the industry. In the coming years, the $10 billion Li-Ion battery market by will be served by six to eight, mostly Asian, manufacturers (NEC/AESC, LG Chem, Panasonic/Sanyo, A123 Systems, SBLiMotive, GSYuasa or Toshiba, likely one/two Chinese). Such a dearth of players is insufficient to drive the kind of cost reductions needed to bring an EV to every garage.

Consumer acceptance is still a challenge

There are more difficulties to deal with. Regretfully, in recent months, consumer confidence in plug-in vehicles has eroded in ways few anticipated. Some of this is due to the expected teething problems in the adoption of new technologies; others due to environmentalists focused on reducing greenhouse gas emissions unhappy about people driving on electricity in those parts of the country where power is generated from coal.[24] But far more disappointing is a round of hatchet jobs against the electric car launched by some on the Right. President Obama's embrace of the technology has made it treif in the eyes of some conservatives. As GM Chairman Daniel Akerson puts it: "Unfortunately, there's one thing we did not engineer. Although we loaded the Volt with state-of-the-art safety features, we did not engineer the Volt to be a political punching bag. And that, sadly, is what it's become."[25] Rush Limbaugh, Glenn Beck, and Fox News' Bill O'Reilly and Neil Cavuto have all portrayed electrified transportation as another expensive government boondoggle and have resorted to four-legs good, two-legs bad thinking.[26] Limbaugh went as far as accusing General Motors of "trying to kill its customers" by selling an unsafe car. Cavuto has repeatedly mocked the Volt in derogatory terms like a "Fred Flintstone car" and "roller skates with a plug." Republican politicians wasted no time responding and took it from there, turning the Volt into a political football. Presidential candidate Newt Gingrich outdid all of them declaring at an embarrassing to watch campaign stop in Georgia: "So let's declare what this election is all about: We believe in the right to bear arms and we'd like to bear arms in our trucks." His punch line: "You can't put a gun rack in a Volt."[27] Come on, Newt, you know better. Talk about a dog whistle. The subtext is that electrified vehicles are for sissy boys while pick-up trucks with gun racks are for manly men. That narrative breaks down with a modicum of a thought, because just like radios, or jumbo tires, or any number of other technologies, hybridization and electrification can be applied to any vehicle platform, from the small to the very large. There is no reason a pickup truck with a gun rack can't be a plug-in hybrid electric vehicle. Indeed, the bigger the vehicle, the more room it has for a battery pack. At the 2012 Chicago Auto show, the Army's Tank Automotive Research, Development and Engineering Center (TARDEC) displayed diesel hybrid tactical vehicles that can climb 60 percent grades, produce over 5,000 foot-pounds of torque, not to mention run silently for eight miles. No, they don't have gun racks, just mounted machine guns.

The problem of sexual stigmatization of energy technologies extends far beyond this single episode. Somewhere in the pandering psychology of American politics, and particularly as it relates to discussions about energy and transportation, certain technologies have been placed into the manly men category while others have gone right into the eunuch bucket. Examples abound: drilling and fracking (manly men) vs., say, biofuels (eunuchs); nuclear (manly men) vs. solar and wind (eunuchs). Instead of a long overdue discussion about policy - when, if at all, should tax credits be used? Should government have the right to issue loan guarantees? Should risks be socialized while returns are not? - this type of demagoguery aims to paint particular technologies − not policies, but technologies − with the broad brush of identity. Some might say "it's just politics." But the danger of such a type of politics is that it shapes consumer perceptions and purchasing choices irreversibly in a way that could have far-reaching economic and national security implications. When the first electric cars appeared on America's roads a century ago, offering a true alternative to the internal combustion engine, they were, like those offered today, clean, odorless, quiet and easy to operate. Yet they were rejected as sissy cars. As author Edwin Black wrote, "Electric cars started with a push of a button but internal combustion vehicles needed strong arms to crank up the car hence it played to the man's masculinity. In that vein, it was commonly thought that electric vehicles appealed to women drivers for their ease of operation, clean running and ladylike start. That sealed it for America's male market."[28] What came next is a century of oil dependency marred with numerous oil wars and interventions, trillions of dollars in economic damage and political deference to the oil cartel. Since then, social stigmas of technologies stalled human progress time and again, causing suffering and loss of lives. This is certainly not unique to the Right. The Left's portrayal of genetically modified crops as Frankenfood diminished their public acceptance in Europe and slowed down – indeed in the case of Africa halted – their penetration to famine stricken countries. There are legitimate grounds to debate the positives and negatives of any new technology, including electric vehicles and non-petroleum fuels in general – cost, safety, performance – but at a time when oil prices are entering a dangerous zone beyond which economic growth could stop, one would hope that pundits and politicians would treat competitors to oil at the very least with a welcoming nod and focus whatever criticism they have on policy and real issues rather than stigmatizing particular technologies as unmanly. Because what starts on the stump or in the studio, ends at the show room.

So what now?

Victims of hyped expectations, high costs and a hostile political climate, electrified vehicles, while tremendously promising, have a long way to go before becoming a permanent fixture in every American garage. It would be foolhardy to ignore other solutions that could proliferate swiftly in the near and mid-term even as slow and steady progress is made in the direction of electrification. The prudent thing to do is therefore to swiftly open cars to a competitive fuel market which takes advantage of America's abundant energy resources – including today's cheap natural gas – to undercut expensive oil, in parallel to steady progress toward vehicle electrification.

5
THE REARDEN METAL OF FUELS

Toxic? I'll drink a jigger of methanol for every two the gasoline people drink.

**C. Boyden Grey, White House Counsel under
President George H. W. Bush. October 5, 1989**

A much touted way to run cars on natural gas is to convert them to burn compressed natural gas (CNG). CNG cars come in two varieties. Some have a dedicated fuel line and a large gas canister in the trunk. They can run solely on natural gas in its gaseous form. Others, bi-fuel vehicles, can run on two fuels: liquid gasoline and gaseous natural gas, stored in separate tanks. The engine in this case can run on one fuel at a time, and drivers are able to switch back and forth between the two. (This is very different concept from flexible fuel vehicles, described later, which store two or more liquid fuels mixed together in the same tank and burn the resulting blend in the combustion chamber.) Adding an entire dedicated fuel system to the vehicle adds thousands of dollars to its cost which is why ready-made CNG cars are barely manufactured by automakers. If one wants to buy a factory built CNG-powered family sedan the only real option for now is the Honda Civic GX, which for several years in a row was voted as the greenest car in America. Its suggested retail price in 2012 was $26,305 when a comparably equipped gasoline-powered Civic was listed for $16,000. Add to that the cost of a home refueling unit – systems retail at approximately $3,000-$4,000, with an installation fee of $1,000-$2,000 – and the pleasure of driving on CNG could easily cost $15,000. GM, Chrysler and Ford offer almost 30 gasoline-only models which can be converted to CNG by qualified system retrofitters, but, here too the cost is prohibitive - $12,000-$18,000, according to Natural Gas Vehicles for America, a group funded by natural gas producers to promote CNG vehicles.[1] The total cost of either a 2011 Chevrolet Express or 2011 GMC Savana Cargo model, which starts at $26,000, would be $41,890 with the CNG option.

In terms of fuel cost, running a car on CNG is significantly cheaper than gasoline: $2.08 per gge for natural gas versus $3.89 per gallon for gasoline in April 2012. But the high incremental cost of the vehicle means the payback period for most Americans would be almost as long as the expected ownership period. (Studies show that payback times of around three years or less are needed for substantial market penetration of costly vehicle technologies.[2]) Under such cost constraints, only high mileage users (over 35,000 miles per year) such as taxis, buses, and garbage trucks are likely to benefit from the option of driving on CNG. For the majority of us the vehicle cost is simply too expensive and over the average vehicle ownership time, the low fuel price doesn't make up for it.

Most of the world's 14.7 million CNG vehicles are found in poor and developing countries like Pakistan, Iran, Brazil, India, Argentina, Uzbekistan, Colombia and Bolivia whereas less than one percent of the world's CNG fleet, 115,000 vehicles, is found in the United States.[3] In Pakistan, 70 percent of light duty vehicles are CNG. How can poor Pakistanis and Iranians afford such an expensive technology? Because their version of it is not expensive. When it comes to CNG vehicles, there is a tradeoff between cost and safety. In Iran, where CNG retrofits are heavily subsidized by the government as a way to encourage drivers to shift from embargoed imported gasoline to domestic natural gas, as in most of the other countries where CNG vehicles are more common, cost saving has taken priority over guarantees of safe performance. The reason people in the developing world can afford to convert their cars to CNG is because they use poor quality components. Their safety standards would not pass muster in the United States. Canisters for CNG cars come in four types, in increasing order of cost and safety: a Type 1 container is made from heavy and cheap steel; Type 2 has a metallic liner over which an overwrap such as carbon fiber or fiberglass is partially applied; a Type 3 container is the same as type 2 just that the overwrap is fully applied over the entire liner, including the domes, and a Type 4 container is plastic gas-tight liner reinforced by composite wrap around the entire tank. This canister is by far the safest and lightest, but four times more expensive than Type 1. According to the National Petroleum Council, current U.S.-based cylinder manufacturers produce Type 3 and 4 products. All Type 1 products, representing 93 percent of the global market for CNG storage tanks, come from foreign suppliers.[4] Malfunctions of a CNG tank caused by poor maintenance, gas leakage, electrical short circuit or a road accident cause in many cases a deadly explosion - the closest thing to a car bomb. Carrying our families on top of a Pakistani-style highly pressurized and poorly maintained Type 1 steel gas canister would, to Americans, be unacceptable. If American consumers were to adopt CNG technology it would have to be done under stringent safety standards and the cost would be in accordance.

An additional challenge for CNG is the need for dedicated refueling infrastructure for gaseous fuel. By April 2012, there were 987 CNG refueling stations nationwide; only 447 of these were open to the public.[5] CNG station construction costs range from $600,000 to $1,700,000 with the average cost being about $750,000.[6] So while compressed natural gas is one of the cheapest and cleanest burning fuels available today, it's not so cheap when the vehicle cost is taken into account. The steep cost for CNG vehicles and refueling infrastructure is what keeps CNG vehicles from penetrating the market en masse. This is why the Energy Information Administration was not optimistic about CNG technology, projecting that light duty CNG vehicles will account for less than 0.1 percent of new vehicle sales by 2035 and heavy duty CNG vehicles will make 1.7 percent.[7] To be sure, some cost reductions may come with mass adoption. But it is difficult to see mass market penetration happening at all unless significant cost reduction comes first. A chicken and egg situation.

On July 8, 2008, with the backdrop of historically high oil prices and with great fanfare, Texas oil billionaire T. Boone Pickens launched a plan he believed would wean America from oil. In a $56 million campaign, Pickens challenged America to substitute wind energy for natural gas used for electricity generation, proclaiming this would free up natural gas to power a third of the vehicles in the United States. (Never mind that nobody gets to unilaterally determine which if any power source for electricity generation is displaced when some other source, whether wind or something else, comes on line. Never mind too that wind power is intermittent, meaning the wind doesn't blow 24/7, and so a utility using wind power will always have backup generators on call in case the wind doesn't supply the goods; those backup generators are generally powered by natural gas, so increased reliance on wind power would mean more, not less, reliance on natural gas-based generation.) At the time, Pickens was heavily invested in wind energy. His giant wind project in the Texas Panhandle was considered the world's biggest wind project. But with the backdrop of the 2009 financial crisis, he suspended the project, and his interest in wind energy apparently blew away. Pickens adjusted his plan, centering his attention on converting the nation's 18-wheelers to run on natural gas instead of diesel. "I'm all American. Any energy in America beats importing," he explained, pushing the New Alternative Transportation to Give American Solutions (NATGAS) Act, a bill crafted in the mold of his plan.[8] NATGAS promised to jump-start natural gas use in vehicles by offering as much as $64,000 in tax credits per natural gas truck purchased as well as other federal provisions from which Pickens' company, Clean Energy Fuels, which sells natural gas to trucks and buses, would be the first in line to gain. The bill, referred to as "Boone-Doggle" by a *Wall Street Journal* editorial, drew a great deal of pushback from fiscal conservatives.[9] Thomas Pyle, President of the American Energy Alliance, wrote "Why compete in the free market when it's more profitable to have Congress do your bidding for you?"[10] Yet more than 180 members of Congress, many of whom call themselves fiscal conservatives, signed up as co-sponsors. In the current climate of fiscal austerity hope is slim for the subsidy laden NATGAS Act. While there is a case to be made under certain circumstances for pushing strategically important brand new technologies out of the barn faster with tax credits geared toward early adopters, it's difficult to justify subsidies for mature technologies whether the CNG vehicle or ethanol.

Liquid solutions

There's another pathway by which natural gas can feed into the transportation fuel market: the liquid option. A range of liquid fuels can be produced from natural gas through thermochemical conversion. But which would be most cost effective and thus have the greatest likelihood of market success?

Liquefied Petroleum Gas (LPG) is a byproduct of natural gas and petroleum, a mixture of propane and butane which today powers more than 150,000 cars in the United States and 15 million worldwide. The U.S. distribution system for LPG is more developed than for CNG - 2,659 stations versus 987.[11] The cost for LPG refueling infrastructure is ten times more affordable than that of CNG, with pumps costing between $45,000 and $60,000. The price could go as high as $175,000 for a large public station. But as with CNG the vehicle conversion cost is high, at $4,000-$12,000.[12] This involves the same consumer acceptance problems discussed above: the value proposition is lacking for the average vehicle owner when the incremental vehicle cost is so high. Furthermore, on a gasoline equivalent basis, the cost of LPG is twice that of CNG, which means consumers have to spend more on the vehicle side without any noticeable payback on the fuel side. Decidedly uninspiring.

Next option: natural gas can be converted into gasoline and diesel. Such "drop-in fuels" seem attractive since they don't necessitate any infrastructure changes or even the slightest vehicle modification. We can use the same cars, trucks, pumps and pipelines without any retrofit. The challenge with gas-to-liquids (GTL) processes is the scale of capital investment they require. The gas-to-gasoline/diesel process is based on Fischer Tropsch synthesis, a technology that was employed as part of Nazi Germany's effort to produce synthetic fuels from coal. In 2011, this technology was applied at a significant commercial scale to natural gas feedstock with the opening of the world's largest GTL plant in Ras Laffan, Qatar. A joint project of Qatar Petroleum and Shell, the plant converts 1.6 billion cubic feet of natural gas into 140,000 barrels a day of petroleum liquids. Oil companies are seriously considering replicating the project elsewhere. North of Nigeria's capital Lagos, Chevron is constructing a much smaller GTL plant. Another GTL plant in Lake Charles Louisiana is now under consideration by the South African Sasol, and a similar size project, also in Louisiana, is being considered by Shell.[13] The capital investment is mind blowing. The estimated price tag of the Louisiana projects is $10 billion each. That was also the cost estimate for the Qatar project. But that estimate was too low and the real cost was eventually more than double, $24 billion.[14] Apart from the absolute cost there is also a question of efficiency (or dollar cost per energy unit of final product, if you will.) As concluded in a Massachusetts Institute of Technology (MIT) report titled *The Future of Natural Gas*, the efficiency of conversion of natural gas into diesel and gasoline is considerably lower – roughly 30 percent lower – than that for the conversion of natural gas to other liquid fuels like mixed alcohols.[15] In fact, one way to make natural gas into diesel or gasoline requires first turning it into liquid alcohol which is then converted further into a drop-in fuel. This additional step requires more energy, more heat, more – much more – natural gas, and the per energy unit cost of the fuel produced is thus higher than the per energy unit cost of the alcohol fuel which is the mid-step product. If vehicles were fuel flexible investors would at least have the option of ending the process mid-way and fueling our cars with the less costly end product, an alcohol called methanol.

The case for methanol

Atlas Shrugged is one of the most widely read books in modern times. Written in 1957 by Ayn Rand, the book details the struggle of Dagny Taggart, an entrepreneurial executive at Taggart Transcontinental, a giant railroad company, against the ever increasing and suffocating control of the government. In an attempt to prevent her company from going under after a string of malfunctions in Taggart Transcontinental's lines, she decides to bet the company's future on Henry Rearden, a self-made steel magnate who developed the strongest and most reliable metal in the world. Against the protests of the steel industry and other defenders of the status quo, Dagny decides to build her new line from Rearden's metal. False claims made by competitors about the alloys are backed by status quo preserving government agencies and Washington lobbyists. And while it becomes clear that the new metal is superior to the conventional one in every respect, Taggart and Rearden soon find themselves fending off lies, fallacies and a well lubricated bureaucracy committed to preventing the new metal from penetrating the market. In today's fuels market, methanol is the equivalent of Rearden metal.

While it enjoys no vocal lobby in Washington or taxpayer funded price support mechanisms, methanol, CH_3OH, is the only high performance liquid fuel that is capable of presenting in the foreseeable future a serious threat to gasoline's hegemony in the fuel market. The reasons methanol holds such great potential for America's energy security are its affordability, its scalability, and the very low cost of enabling vehicles to use it. Flexible fuel cars that can interchangeably use gasoline and a variety of alcohols, including methanol, blending them all in one fuel tank, cost automakers about $100 more to manufacture as compared to gasoline only cars, as we discuss at length in Chapter 8. Both volumetrically (in other words gallon for gallon) as well as on a cents-per-mile basis methanol is cheaper than gasoline. The July 2012 global spot price for methanol made from natural gas was $1.15 per gallon, without any subsidy and with a very substantial mark up over production cost.

Methanol contains about half the energy of gasoline per gallon, but this doesn't mean it takes twice as much fuel to go the same distance. Methanol is utilized much more efficiently by engines because of its lower heat output – that means less energy is wasted, stretching a dollar of fuel purchase further. Methanol also has a much higher octane rating than gasoline (108 vs. gasoline's 85) and can be used in cars with higher compression ratios. An effective measure of the methanol-gasoline miles per gallon ratio would therefore be 1:1.6 (see Chapter 6.) While standard vehicles will see a mileage loss per gallon, methanol's low cost means they will save money per mile as compared to using gasoline. Car design in the future could take advantage of high octane to achieve near mile per gallon parity with gasoline.

Methanol can be made today competitively, with existing technology, from energy resources with which the United States is well endowed -

natural gas, coal, biomass, garbage or any other organic material. In the future, perhaps even recycled carbon dioxide could be commercially converted into methanol, providing an elegant solution to the otherwise seemingly economically irresolvable issue of fossil fuels-derived greenhouse gas emissions. Methanol was first produced as a minor byproduct of producing charcoal from wood and was therefore called wood alcohol. In the 19th century, before the appearance of kerosene, methanol was used for lighting, cooking, and heating purposes. Until the 1920s, wood was the only source for methanol. After World War I, Germany began producing methanol from coal, and after World War II, natural gas became the preferred feedstock. Today, methanol is one of the most commonly used chemicals. It goes into our windshield washer fluid; it is commonly applied as a solvent and as antifreeze in pipes; it is used in wastewater treatment plants and as power booster in high performance diesel engines. It is even used in the production and commercialization of other fuels like biodiesel and ethanol. Where it is not used directly – and should be allowed to be – is in our fuel tank. Just like Rearden metal, despite its potential, methanol is largely unknown, politically an orphan and too often unjustifiably denigrated.

Methanol from natural gas – a low hanging fruit

Today, about two thirds of the worldwide production of methanol is derived from natural gas. In fact, the aforementioned MIT study determined that methanol is the most economically viable way to utilize natural gas in transportation due to its low cost and mature production and vehicle technology. It estimated that on an energy equivalent basis the production cost of natural gas conversion to methanol is 30 percent lower than the gas-to-diesel process and that it would also result in a 50 percent reduction in greenhouse gas emissions.[16]

It takes roughly 100 cubic feet of natural gas to produce a gallon of methanol. So if natural gas is priced at $3 per thousand cubic feet (which is about the same as $3/mmbtu) the cost of the natural gas which goes into each gallon of methanol adds up to about 40 cents. Fixed and variable costs add up to another 11 cents per gallon. Both the MIT analysis and a report by the Baker Institute predict U.S. gas prices in the $6-$8/mmbtu range for the coming two decades.[17] This is the price range against which we should test the economic viability of methanol. Six-dollar gas would drive the natural gas input cost to roughly 60 cents, and $8 gas to roughly 80 cents. In other words, the production cost of a gallon of methanol at $3 gas is about 51 cents, at $6 gas about 71 cents, and at $8 gas about 91 cents not including financing, depreciation, or taxes. That means that even if natural gas prices were to double or triple as compared with summer 2012 prices, methanol would still be competitive with gasoline, as long as oil price is above $45-$50 a barrel.

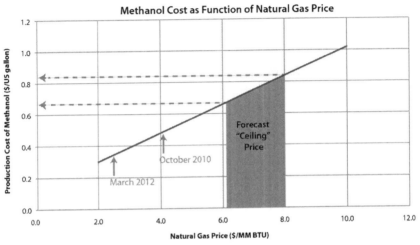

Production cost of methanol as a function of natural gas prices

Source: Vikram Rao

Whether or not investors expand the domestic methanol industry, it is expected that over time the wide spread between oil and natural gas prices will begin to close. If natural gas demand builds up, prices will be pushed upward, but the same will happen even if it doesn't. If demand stays stagnant, natural gas producers that are unprofitable at the current price band will have no choice but to scale back production. With less supply, prices will climb. Between the two scenarios, the first is much more desirable for the economy. If natural gas prices are to go up there will at least be a benefit of productive economic activity, domestic investment, and competition against oil, not to mention lots of jobs created along the way. Under the second scenario, we will continue to import increasingly expensive oil to power our automobiles while our natural gas remains in the ground.

The world has so many plentiful energy resources from which methanol can be made that the fuel can give gasoline and thus oil a real run for the money. Natural gas is one of the most attractive sources. Suppose that only ten percent of the roughly 2.5 quadrillion cubic feet of U.S. recoverable natural gas resources were to be used for transportation. That would generate 2.5 trillion gallons of methanol that could be blended into our fuel supply, an amount equivalent to 11 years of U.S. gasoline demand. Another way to understand the potential: Since the beginning of the shale gas boom the American natural gas industry has ramped up production by roughly 1.5 trillion cubic feet per year. If just that additional gas were to be used as automotive fuel that would be enough to add the equivalent of 10 billion gallons of gasoline to America's fuel mix. How many plants would be needed to reach a 10 billion gallon capacity? What would be the capital investment? A 600 million gallon per year mega-methanol plant costs roughly $1.2 billion. It would therefore take 16 large plants at a cumulative cost of $19 billion, less than what it cost to build Ras Laffan at double the energy equivalent fuel production.

Table 5.1: Methanol/Gasoline production cost comparison
(gallon of gasoline equivalent, gge, April 2012)[18]

Natural gas price ($/mmbtu)	Methanol production cost per gallon	Methanol production cost per gge	Production cost (crude refining) of a gallon of gasoline which retails for $4/g	Production cost reduction per gge of methanol compared to gasoline
$3	$0.51	$1.02	2.96	$1.94
$4	$0.61	$1.22	2.96	$1.74
$6	$0.71	$1.42	2.96	$1.54
$8	$0.91	$1.82	2.96	$1.14

In his book *Shale Gas: The Promise and the Peril,* Vikram Rao, the former CTO of Haliburton, makes the point that methanol will eliminate much of the volatility from the transportation market. His argument: "Gasoline price will always be driven by world events, whereas methanol will be largely regional, so stability in that commodity will at least keep *cost* under control."[19] It is also worth remembering that markets are unpredictable and one cannot be certain how new technologies might shape the demand curve for natural gas. In fact, under some scenarios natural gas prices could drop even further. For example in May 2012, the Department of Energy announced a breakthrough in research into the tapping of methane hydrates.[20] These crystal-like structures containing natural gas are found on the bottom of the ocean in gigantic quantities. While work on methane hydrates is in a very early stage, if it indeed becomes possible at some point to unlock this resource, it would render the shale gas revolution a footnote. But because natural gas is only one of several sources of energy that can be used as feedstock for methanol production, the future of methanol is not tied exclusively to natural gas. A great deal of methanol can be made from other sources.

Coal-derived methanol

Long before the United States was referred to by President Obama as the Saudi Arabia of natural gas, it was described by many as the Saudi Arabia of coal. Not that being compared with Saudi Arabia is exactly a badge of honor, but the point is that America is loaded with fossil fuels of all types and coal is the most abundant of all. But this coal is used almost exclusively in the electricity sector. More than a full third of our nation's electricity is made of it. Now, the emergence of electric vehicles provides an opportunity for coal to move people and goods for the first time since the decline of coal fired steam engines in trains and ships. As described in the previous chapter, however, electrification might take a while. If lique-fied, coal can play a role in transportation today. In 1925, Franz Fischer and Hans Tropsch used an indirect liquefaction process, which still bears their name, to produce excellent transportation fuels. During World War II, Germany had 25 liquefaction plants that produced more than 124,000 barrels daily of synthetic petroleum product and met 90 percent of the nation's needs. The process also served South Africa well during the apartheid years. But in the rest of the world the technology has not attracted many followers. The main reason has been cost. The capital investment required to build a coal-to-liquids plant with a capacity of 80,000 barrels per day could reach $10 billion, just like GTL. As long as oil stayed under $50 a barrel such plants made little economic sense. Even today, when oil prices seem to be permanently high, coal-to-liq-uids refineries are considered a high risk endeavor and very few countries outside of China are interested in pursuing this option. The economics are far more appealing when coal is used in a different process to make methanol. As we describe in the next chapter, coal to methanol capacity has grown rapidly in China. The process converts coal into synthesis gas (that's carbon monoxide and hydrogen) and then the syngas is converted further into alcohol. Producing one million gallons of methanol using this method requires about 5,000 short tons of coal. So five percent of the current U.S. annual coal production of one billion short tons, or roughly half the amount of coal the United States currently exports would yield 10 billion gallons of methanol.[21] The conversion of coal to methanol is particularly appealing since cheap low grade coal can be used.

Environmentally friendly fuel

Natural gas and coal make perfect feedstock for methanol production, but it would be wrong to assume that methanol is necessarily a fossil fuel-derived solution or that methanol is detrimental to the environment. The exact opposite is true. Methanol's debut in the United States in the 1990's was mostly driven by air quality considerations. Methanol produces much less nitrogen oxide (NOx) pollution than gasoline, and because it contains no sulfur it does not produce sulfur dioxide at all. It also reduces ground-level ozone smog in urban centers. Unregulated emissions like formaldehyde normally increase with the use of methanol, but the use of a conventional three-way catalyst can reduce both regulated and unregulated emissions to the same levels as those generated by a conventional gasoline engine.

Methanol also offers significant benefits in preventing underground water pollution. This is why on June 12, 1989 President George H.W. Bush announced a major alternative fuel vehicle program which included 500,000 methanol vehicles for 1996, 750,000 for 1997, and one million per year after that. Federal and state governments were required to purchase alternative fuel vehicles for their fleets. The plan was not implemented as rapidly as planned but by the late 1990s, there were more than 17,000 methanol compatible cars on the road, most of them in California. Ten automakers were involved in the effort including GM, Chrysler, Toyota, Volkswagen, Nissan and Mercedes. Many of the cars were developed by Ford, including the 1.6L Escort, the 3.0L Taurus, the 5.0L Crown Victoria and the 5.0L Econoline vans. The cars were sold without any price premium compared to their gasoline-only counterparts. ARCO, Texaco, Mobil, Chevron, Shell, Exxon and Ultramar (now Shell) opened some of their stations to methanol, offering M85 blends.

But the introduction of reformulated gasoline by the oil companies reduced the air quality benefit of methanol vis-à-vis gasoline and thus much of California's interest in the fuel. More importantly, oil prices in the 1990s were so low and natural gas so high that there was not the economic rationale that there is today to shift from an oil product to a natural gas derived product. The late Roberta Nichols, the head honcho of Ford's alternative fuels program and a methanol enthusiast who raced a methanol-powered 1929 Model A Ford at 190 miles per hour at the Bonneville Salt Flats in Utah, summed it up: "By the middle of the decade, energy security was no longer on the "radar screen" [...] Gasoline was cheap, plentiful, and reformulated."[22]

Today, air and water quality benefits are no longer the prime concern of the environmental movement. After scoring one victory after another in cleaning our air and water this movement has changed its focus in recent years to sharply reducing carbon dioxide emissions from vehicles and power plants. When it comes to greenhouse gas emissions, methanol's "well-to-wheel" CO_2 emissions are lower than gasoline's if the methanol is produced from natural gas, sharply lower if the methanol is made from renewable sources, and higher if it is made from coal. In Germany, Schwarze Pumpe produces 100,000 tons of methanol from sewage sludge and industrial wastes each year. In Sweden, methanol is made from black liquor, a sludge byproduct of paper pulping. And in Reykjavik, Iceland, in 2012 the world's first industrial scale plant to produce renewable methanol from CO_2 was opened by a company called Carbon Recycling International. The company has announced tentative plans to build an additional plant in Northern Iceland which would produce over 25 million gallons of methanol annually. The idea of using CO_2 as a raw material that can be made into usable products makes much more economic sense than the much touted vision of carbon sequestration - capturing CO_2 collected in power stations and injecting it into deep underground rock formations and storage sites with the hope that it will stay there forever. The problem with sequestration is that it imposes significant costs that consumers will have to pay, should the technology become commercialized and widely applied, for capturing, transporting and disposing of each molecule of CO_2 they helped emit. Such an indulgence can at best be entertained by rich societies, not ones facing the specter of economic meltdown. Converting CO_2 into methanol – that is, treating CO_2 as a resource from which products can be made rather than as a waste product which must be disposed of at high cost - offers a market large enough to absorb the billions of tons of CO_2 we emit every year. But how can it be done?

Nobel Laureate in Chemistry Professor George Olah has been a proponent of converting CO_2 into methanol in a process that resembles photosynthesis – a closed loop cycle in which every molecule of CO_2 released by burning methanol on board an automobile would be cancelled out by a similar molecule captured to make it. Olah is co-inventor of the direct methanol fuel cell, which uses methanol to generate electricity, with the byproducts of CO_2 and water. While developing the concept, it occurred to him and his team that the process can be reversed. CO_2 from sources where it is present in high concentrations, like flue gases from a power plant burning natural gas, could be combined with water, using electric power, to form methanol. Eventually, Olah believes we could just take CO_2 out of the air. Industry is beginning to express interest in this approach. In May 2009, the Japanese Mitsui Chemical Inc. began operating a pilot plant for production of methanol from industrial CO_2 effluent and photocatalyst produced hydrogen.[23] The challenge is to chemically reduce carbon dioxide into carbon monoxide, a building block for fuel. This is not a simple process. CO_2 is a clingy molecule, and the carbon-oxygen bond requires a reliable catalyst to break it. If CO_2 is heated to 1,700°C, it splits into carbon monoxide and oxygen, which can be catalyzed into methanol. But what source of energy could be used to generate such heat without emitting more CO_2 into the atmosphere? Olah puts his faith in nuclear power. Others believe that energy from concentrated solar power can do the trick. Researchers at Sandia National Laboratories in New Mexico, for example, use sunlight through a chamber containing mirrors to divide CO_2 into carbon monoxide and oxygen. For now, these processes are in the development stage as low energy catalysts are sought and it might take decades before they fully mature. But there are mature processes which allow the production of renewable methanol today from a resource with which the United States is extremely well endowed – biomass.

Biomass: Chemistry beats biology

In his 2006 State of the Union Address President George W. Bush hyped wood chips as a source for cellulosic ethanol that would break America's addiction to oil, pledging that with government funding cellulosic ethanol would be "practical and competitive within six years."

Shortly after that, on May 16, 2006, legendary Silicon Valley venture capitalist Vinod Khosla testified before the Senate proposing "a Marshall Plan for our times that would support technological advancements and sustainable development of a global alternative to petroleum [...] and best of all it takes very little money to do." His solution, cellulosic ethanol, was slated to deliver all that. "We can be irreversibly traveling down this path in less than seven years," he concluded.[24] A great deal of money has been invested in technologies to convert cellulose to ethanol using enzymes and other genetically modified biocatalysts and numerous cellulosic ethanol ventures sprang up like mushrooms after the rain, many of which relied on tax dollar handouts. To ensure a market for the fuel, in 2007, in a Soviet central planning style move, Congress mandated that the United States use 100 million gallons of cellulosic ethanol yearly by 2010, and 250 million gallons by 2011—though not a single commercial facility existed at the time. This as industry spokesmen have for years insisted that we are just a few months away from commercialization. The process involves a few fundamental phases. Microbes break long chains of cellulose molecules into sugars. The sugar solution is then separated from the residual materials and fermented into alcohol. In nature, these processes are performed by different enzymes and microbes. Cellulosic ethanol visionaries try to create a "bug of all trades," one that can break down cellulose like a bacterium, ferment sugar like yeast and tolerate high concentrations of alcohol (alcohol is a killer if over-consumed). Such super bugs are extremely difficult to engineer, requiring the manipulation of many genes, but the payback could be fantastic, which explains why so many high profile tech-investors are pouring millions into this burgeoning industry. But despite the enthusiasm of some politicians and venture capitalists, cellulosic biomass feedstocks don't easily give up their starches, and the technologies needed to ferment cellulose in high-pressure chambers that have limited amounts of oxygen are expensive and rudimentary. Just like President Bush's previous fad, the hydrogen economy, cellulosic ethanol has thus far failed to live up to its promise. Khosla's great cellulosic hope, Cello Energy, filed for bankruptcy in 2010. His other venture, Range Fuels, which in 2007 received a $76 million grant from the Department of Energy, ended up as a fiasco with nothing to show for itself.

The lesson is not that biomass cannot be made economically into fuel. It can be. According to the DOE's Oak Ridge National Lab there are enough agriculture and forest resources to potentially produce at least one billion dry tons of biomass annually, in a sustainable manner—enough to replace approximately 30 percent of the country's present petroleum consumption.[25] The question is at what cost and with what technology?

The failure of the cellulosic ethanol experiment stems from the fact is was essentially a politically directed investment. Simply put: industry was told by government that only one product is to be made from biomass and that is ethanol. And industry, we know, follows incentives. If federal tax dollar grants supported only banana peels-to-ethanol processes, you could bet that technology would gravitate toward this exact pathway and that our government would soon be bombarded by self-serving pleas from superrich investors who want taxpayers to finance their attempts to become even richer. More likely to succeed than the cellulose-to-ethanol initiative would have been a cellulose-to-fuel effort without government constraints on what type of process should be used or what type of liquid fuel emerges from the process. If that was the case, we would today have probably had a flourishing cellulosic biofuels industry that does not rely on cutting edge scientific developments. It would be based on methanol.

While biology is still in its early stages, chemistry is ready to rumble. There are multiple available ways to chemically convert biomass into fuel including combustion, gasification and pyrolysis, each with its own requirement of heat, pressure and time. Methanol provides an easier and more efficient way to convert biomass into liquid fuel that does not require the invention of new organisms. (The well-known industrial process of making methanol from biomass, with its unexciting industrial rates of return on investment isn't so appealing if you're looking for Google scale returns. VCs focused on this space sought blockbuster bugs to patent and license, not well known technology for cookie cutter replication, and Congressional staffers thus heard a steady drumbeat of cellulosic ethanol talk from them.) Methanol is called wood alcohol because it was first produced from pyrolysis of wood. In this process, the biomass material, which essentially includes everything that is or used to be a plant, including the book you are holding (unless of course you happen to be reading this electronically) is usually dried, pulverized and then pressurized and heated to a temperature of 800°F in the absence of oxygen to allow complete combustion. The resulting gas contains a mixture of carbon monoxide, hydrogen, carbon dioxide and water vapor. This syngas is sent to a methanol producing unit where, going through a series of catalysts, purified and separated from the water, it becomes a usable liquid fuel. This process was introduced by the German chemical company BASF as early as the 1920s.[26] The production cost is roughly a dollar per gallon, significantly higher than the 40 cents that it costs to turn natural gas to methanol at the current below \$3 per mmbtu natural gas prices.[27] But compared to cellulosic ethanol the process is hugely efficient: one ton of dry wood can be converted into 165-185 gallons of methanol. So we can compare apples to apples the same amount of energy as contained in 123-138 gallons of ethanol. If the same ton of biomass were converted into ethanol using an enzymatic process (i.e., to cellulosic ethanol) it would yield only 90 gallons. Another beauty of gasification is that it is feedstock agnostic. The gasifier does not care whether it is fed by forest residue, paper waste or corn stover. It handles them all. Biological processes are not nearly as versatile. The bugs are super picky and know how to digest only one dedicated feedstock stream. Of course, the efficiency of the process depends on the level of moisture and impurities each feedstock has, but generally speaking, the gasifier can handle not only every form of biomass but also coal, another resource with which the United States is blessed.

Table 5.2: Summary of currently used and potential forest and agriculture biomass at \$60 per dry ton or less, under baseline scenario assumptions (million dry tons per year)

Feedstock	2012	2017	2022	2030
Forest resources currently used	129	182	210	226
Forest biomass & waste resource potential	97	98	100	102
Agricultural resources currently used	85	103	103	103
Agricultural biomass & waste resource potential	162	192	221	265
Energy crops	0	101	282	400
Total currently used	214	284	312	328
Total potential resources	258	392	602	767
Total	473	676	914	1094

Source: U.S. Department of Energy

How much methanol can be made from biomass? In theory, the projected one billion tons of available biomass per year could generate as much as 170-180 billion gallons of methanol per year which would be enough to replace half of America's gasoline consumption by 2030. In the real world the lion's share of our forest residue and biomass waste would be uneconomical to collect and liquefy. But if only one tenth of America's biomass endowment were converted into liquid fuel, that would more than double America's existing biofuels production capacity.

All of this is to say that to those focused on the environment methanol offers many interesting opportunities both in terms of its ability to reduce greenhouse gas emissions as well as clean our air and water. As we can see in Table 5.4 unless the methanol is made from coal, we are likely to experience decreased carbon intensity compared to gasoline. The decrease would be slight if natural gas is the main feedstock and significant if a renewable source is used. Furthermore, methanol production processes are moving in the opposite direction as those of oil. Today methanol is mostly made from fossil fuels but just like electricity as the years go by if the economics make sense it can increasingly become a renewable fuel, a product of non-fossil fuels. In other worlds, methanol will become greener over time. Gasoline, on the other hand, will forever be a product of fossils, and as oil prices rise and tar sands and oil shale become increasingly economic its carbon intensity will only grow.

Table 5.3: Lifetime carbon intensity in gram/MJfuel[28]

Reformulated gasoline	96
CNG	68
Corn ethanol	68
Electricity (CA average)	124
Methanol from NG in FFV	67
Methanol from coal	190
Methanol from coal with CCS	89
Methanol from renewables	5

Methane: catch it if you can

Those concerned about greenhouse gas emissions should stop and think about methane (CH_4), the main component of natural gas. Methane emitted into the atmosphere traps 72 times more heat than carbon dioxide. A great deal of methane is emitted by livestock and landfills, but about a third of the world's emissions of methane occur in coal mines and natural gas wells, where billions of cubic feet of natural gas are currently being flared by oil companies. According to the World Bank sponsored Global Gas Flaring Reduction Partnership, a total amount of 5.3 trillion cubic feet of natural gas is being flared annually, equivalent to 25 percent of U.S. gas consumption or 75 percent of Russia's gas exports.[29] Flaring is a global problem. Iraq flares more than half the gas it produces. Gas flaring from Nigerian wells and refineries alone emits more greenhouse gases than any other single source in Africa south of the Sahara. Iran and Russia also flare a great deal of gas. But no one thought that the United States would ever make it to the unflattering list of the world's top ten gas flaring nations. With North Dakota becoming America's fourth largest oil and gas producing state, we joined the club. In North Dakota alone, more than 100 million cubic feet of natural gas are being flared daily.[30] "North Dakota is not as bad as Kazakhstan, but this is not what you would expect a civilized, efficient society to do: to flare off a perfectly good product just because it's expensive to bring to market," said Michael E. Webber, associate director of the Center for International Energy and Environmental Policy at the University of Texas at Austin.[31] Methanol enables the United States to capture and monetize flared methane. In Equatorial Guinea, for example, gas that had been previously flared is being turned into 300 million gallons of methanol per year. There is opportunity for that to happen elsewhere; certainly in the United States. Using about 10 percent of the world's flared natural gas would produce 50 billion gallons of methanol - enough to fuel fifty million cars. If captured at the wellhead and turned into methanol, North Dakota's flared methane alone could make a million gallons of fuel every single working day.

Methanol myths and facts

Just like Rearden's metal, methanol's virtues as a product have been deliberately underappreciated. The introduction of a new fuel may be good for most Americans, but for some legacy businesses, more fuel choice means new headaches. The California experiment demonstrated how fierce the opposition of the oil industry can be to wide distribution of non-petroleum fuel.[32] Today, it is not only the automakers, refiners and fuel distributers that oppose the fuel but also some ethanol interests, who view methanol with trepidation, fearing that it will compete with their product over the capped additive market share. (big fish in a small pond mentality, as discussed in Chapter 7) The easiest way to kill any product is to question its safety. And indeed methanol has been portrayed as a deadly poison that has no room in our surroundings. Reality check: windshield washer fluid contains 10-25 percent methanol. Such fluids are being used daily; they are being sprayed into the environment, occasionally come in touch with our skin and no one frets over this exposure. If we can spray methanol on our windshields why can't we put it in our tank? True, when a large quantity is swallowed, the alcohol is broken down to formaldehyde and formic acid, both toxic materials, and the reaction could lead to blindness, coma and death. But hey, it is fuel we are talking about, not a beverage. In reality, unless swallowed, methanol is quite benign. Our bodies contain methanol naturally, and many items in our diet, including fresh fruit, have methanol in them. Aspartame from fermented foods and beverages is converted into methanol in our body almost every day of our lives. Your body is likely to absorb more methanol from drinking a glass of orange juice than from fueling a car with methanol.

Those who dismiss methanol as poison ignore an important fact - gasoline is toxic too. Open any car manual and see the warning: "Gasoline is highly toxic and if swallowed can cause death or permanent injury." Indeed, deaths have been reported from ingestion of less than one ounce of gasoline yet none of these toxic properties have stopped us from using trillions of gallons of gasoline over a century. When it comes to safety, methanol is actually safer than gasoline. Gasoline contains aromatics like benzene, which is a cancer-causing agent. Methanol doesn't. Gasoline is highly flammable, causing hundreds of deaths a year from car fires. Methanol burns 75 percent slower than gasoline, and its fire releases heat at one-eighth the rate of gasoline. It is much more difficult to ignite than gasoline, and much less likely to cause deadly fires. The Environmental Protection Agency (EPA) estimated that switching fuels from gasoline to methanol would reduce the annual incidence of fuel related fires by 90 percent, saving an estimated 720 lives, preventing nearly 3,900 serious injuries, and eliminating property losses of millions of dollars a year."[33] Methanol fires can be extinguished with water, whereas gasoline floats on water and continues to burn. Ask the Indy 500 drivers who for this reason, not to mention its high octane, for decades used methanol as their fuel of choice.

One completely off base anti-methanol claim circulated by the Auto Alliance is that if it is accidentally released from leaking underground fuel storage tanks it may contaminate well water. This claim confuses methanol with MTBE (methyl tertiary butyl ether), the additive made from methanol that did contaminate groundwater and was eventually banned. But methanol is not MTBE. Blaming methanol for the sins of MTBE is like blaming paper for the sins of cigarettes. An accidental release of methanol would cause much less damage than a comparable gasoline or crude oil spill. Had the Exxon Valdez that collided with Bligh Reef in March 1989 been loaded with methanol, instead of crude oil, the effects of the accident would have disappeared within 3-5 days.[34] The reason: methanol is totally soluble in water, and would be rapidly diluted to a concentration low enough for microorganisms to start biodegradation. Indeed, methanol is used for denitrification in water treatment plants as a food for bacteria.[35]

Another common line of attack: methanol corrodes certain metals, such as magnesium and aluminum as well as rubber, polyurethane, and most plastics. True. Methanol is corrosive. So are gasoline and ethanol. To address corrosion one must use higher grade materials in the fuel line which are compatible with the degree of corrosion methanol presents. Carmakers have been introducing those materials at no additional cost. As we will see in the next chapter, in low blends, (under 15 percent) methanol can be used in existing vehicles. In higher blends, one should not use methanol in a non-flexible fuel vehicle. The good news is that no special fabrication techniques are necessary to produce methanol fuel systems for flexible fuel vehicles. In fact, most of the materials used today have been proven to be compatible with methanol. Unfortunately the flexible-fuel vehicles presently sold in the United States are not warrantied to operate on methanol. Were Congress to enact an Open Fuel Standard, ensuring that new cars sold in America that have an internal combustion engine are flex fuel and that fuel flexibility includes all alcohols, not only ethanol, the door would be opened to a competitive liquid fuels market.

Table 5.4: Comparison of natural gas uses in transportation:
CNG vs. methanol FFV

	CNG	Methanol FFV
Vehicle	Extra $10,000-$15,000 to retrofit a regular gasoline car.	Roughly $100 extra to the cost of an equivalent gasoline-powered car. After market conversion: $400-$1,000
Refueling infrastructure	Single pump installation: $600,000-$1,700,000 Home refueling system: around $4,500	Single pump retrofit: $15,000-$20,000 New pump with storage tank: $60,000
Fuel cost (July 2012)	$2.13 for a gasoline gallon equivalent (gge) of fuel.	$3.13 per gge
Refueling time and convenience	Few minutes at the station Home refueling units: 4 hours after 50 miles of driving or 16 hours if the tank is completely empty.	Few minutes
Greenhouse gas emissions: % change vs. petroleum fuel displaced	-28%	-8% However, an FFV platform enables use of: •Cellulosic ethanol -91% •Sugar ethanol -56% •Corn ethanol -22% •Methanol from biomass -50%

Convenience	Reduced trunk space	No change
Range	About half the range of gasoline in all scenarios	About half the range of gasoline if run on pure methanol but allows range flexibility if lower blends are used. Optimized, high-compression engines can attain mileage equivalency with gasoline.
Energy security	-No fuel flexibility -Problems in domestic supply would entail import from unfriendly sources -Reliance on domestic resource	-Full fuel flexibility: Methanol can also be made from other sources (coal, biomass) -Methanol FFV can also run on other alcohols as well as on gasoline -Many countries have potential for alcohol production.
Safety	Relatively safe, unless goes on fire	Fuel is toxic when swallowed – don't drink! Otherwise safe. Harder to ignite than gasoline and burns with one-eighth the heat – meaning less risk of injury and damage from accidents, fires.

Sources: Methanol Institute, Natural Gas Vehicles for America, National Petroleum Council, Natural Resources Defense Council

The ace in the deck

Methanol's scalability, its environmental benefits and the relative easiness in which it can enter the market are the main reasons why it should be closely studied. Highly competitive and environmentally friendly, it does not necessitate the significant investments required in changes of vehicle platforms as in the case of EVs and in vehicles and distribution systems as in the case of CNG. Production of methanol from multiple resources is an important asset to energy security as it guarantees that no more would America's transportation sector be beholden to the travails of one energy feedstock or the other. In the United States and the world at large, a significant resource endowment of natural gas, coal and biomass, could be used to produce enormous amounts of methanol. But much of this production will not occur if cars are not open to the fuel.

Table 5.5: U.S. national annual potential for methanol production

	gge in billion gallons	Resource dedicated to methanol
Natural gas	13.75	One tenth of domestic production
Coal	12.50	One tenth of domestic production
Biomass	5.25	One tenth of domestic production
Flared methane	0.50	Entire domestic resource
Total	32.00	

Competition over transportation fuel market share among gasoline, methanol, and other fuels would yield competition over price with downward pressure on oil prices. To be sure, there are challenges to the introduction of a new fuel into the marketplace – adjustment of supply chains, consumer education, EPA approval, engine adjustments and infrastructure retrofits to name a few – but none of them are show stoppers. Roberta Nichols summarized the California experience as follows: "Successful introduction of methanol has some fundamental requirements. There must be an adequate number of refueling stations, the price of the fuel must be stable, and the fuel quality must be controlled. Most important of all, it is not likely that anything will happen unless the oil industry is a partner in the overall objectives and action plan."[36] A visit to the People's Republic of China, the world's beta site for methanol blending, can teach us how one country is meeting these challenges.

6
METHANOL ECONOMY'S BETA SITE

It takes ten years to sharpen a sword.

Chinese proverb

With a population larger than that of California, Shanxi province is the hub of China's coal industry. Home to some of China's most polluted cities, the northern province is hardly a top tourist attraction. But for those interested in energy security, it is a fascinating place to explore as Shanxi is today the Mecca of methanol blending. If one wants to see what a methanol economy might look like on a large scale, Shanxi, and in particular its capital, Taiyuan, is the place to be. Shuttling between the Provincial Museum, the beautiful Twin Pagoda Temple and the Liu Xiang, the popular food street in Taiyuan, or the nearby picturesque and ancient city of Pingyao, a visitor might not notice that the city's buses, taxis and many private vehicles run on methanol. They do. Throughout the province, methanol is omnipresent. Light duty vehicles fuel regularly with M15 (A blend of 15 percent methanol and 85 percent gasoline); most taxis as well as numerous buses and commercial vehicles run on M85 and M100. Chinese like the ability to use a cleaner fuel and one that is substantially cheaper per mile than gasoline. Outside of Shanxi, methanol is now blended and tested in one capacity or another in 25 out of China's 31 provinces including the provinces of Shanghai, Shaanxi, Hebei, Henan, Jiangsu, Zhejiang and Guizhou. To support the fleet of methanol cars, an entire system of fuel production, blending and distribution has emerged. China has more than 200 methanol factories nationwide; ten local standards on methanol fuel have been published; and in Shanxi Province alone, more than 1,200 service stations offer methanol blends. This number is slated to double by 2015. The rise of methanol in China has been meteoric. Production capacity has grown from 2 billion gallons in 2003 to nearly 15 billion gallons today, about the size of America's ethanol industry. Within less than a decade, China's methanol use in the transportation sector grew from virtually zero to a point it replaced more than eight percent of the country's gasoline demand. In the next couple of years, more than 200,000 additional vehicles will be converted to use methanol in addition to the existing 150,000, and 50,000 methanol fueled heavy duty trucks will be introduced.[1] Shanxi Province is also planning to add additional blends and use a billion gallons in new blends like M30 and M50. This is only the beginning. But how did it all happen?

Ford's gift to China

Researchers in Shanxi began experimenting with methanol as early as the beginning of the 1980s, including the deployment of demonstration fleets, testing of various blends and developing catalysts and engine parts to ensure optimal performance of methanol cars. In 1993, China became a net oil importer and with concerns about energy security surfacing, the curiosity about fuels that could compete with gasoline and diesel turned into an imperative. At the time there were only six million vehicles in China. But China's planners knew that if their country were to follow the growth pattern of other Asian tigers, dependency on a volatile global oil market – not to mention on a resource shipped through sea lanes where China didn't have a serious presence - would soon become the country's greatest economic bottleneck. The situation was begging for an urgent and aggressive effort to secure its oil supply and in parallel for an equally determined non-petroleum fuels program. What was less clear was the type of fuel China should pursue. Electric cars were immature; China has no significant reserve of conventional natural gas so natural gas vehicles were not really an option, and ethanol and biodiesel from food crops were not an exciting solution for Chinese planners fully cognizant of a growing and potentially restless urban population which is accustomed to low prices for food staples. But China has the world's third largest coal reserve after the United States and Russia and more than half of its reserve is low grade coal. If there was only a way to turn this resource into an affordable transportation fuel, energy security would be greatly enhanced. Methanol seemed to be the answer.

Seeking solutions that could be implemented on a large scale, the central regime in Beijing took interest in Shanxi's experiments with methanol. What firmed the planners' faith in methanol was the fact that at the very same time the United States too was toying with the fuel.[2] In the autumn of 1995, as the United States was in the middle of its methanol blending program in California, a group of Chinese academics and government officials came for a visit. Turning China's vast coal deposits into methanol would be a win-win-win situation, they thought. It would reduce the Middle Kingdom's oil vulnerability, clean up the air and find a high value usage for China's low grade coal. With this insight in mind, officials from the Chinese Ministry of Technology and Science, the Beijing-based Tsinghua University, and the Chinese Academy of Sciences, China's national scientific think tank, joined forces with MIT, Volkswagen and Ford Motor Company, at the time the leader in methanol cars. A study conducted jointly by those institutions concluded that coal based methanol was the most natural choice for Shanxi Province and other coal-rich regions. As part of the cooperation, Ford gave Shanxi a gift - a methanol enabled vehicle. This gift allowed the Shanxi-based Datong Automobile Factory to produce China's first indigenous methanol automobile, leading to a series of national and provincial methanol automobile projects. One of the driving forces behind the initiative was He Guangyuan, who was China's Minister of Machinery and Electronics Industry in 1989-1993. Guangyuan was so outspoken in his support for methanol that the Chinese media dubbed him the 'minister of methanol.' It was he who recommended the advancement of methanol fuel to China's President Hu Jintao and Premier Wen Jiabao after their taking office in 2003.[3] Another convert was Vice Premier Li Keqiang, speculated to be China's next premier. In 2005, the national government approved a project which involved the engine conversions of 100 buses and 200 taxis. In September 2006, eight leaders from China's coal-producing provinces provided a report to President Hu titled "Suggestion on Promoting Methanol Fuels to Replace Gasoline and Diesel Fuel." Hu approved their recommendations and directed the National Development and Reform Commission (NDRC), the powerful arm of the Chinese government for macroeconomic planning, to explore the use of methanol fuels. It didn't take long for the NDRC to see the potential of methanol for China's energy security and order the development of national methanol fuel blending standards.

It also didn't take long for the all-powerful forces of China's oil industry to kick into high gear and try to block the initiative. For obvious reasons, China's Big Oil had no taste for competition at its pumps. The state-owned Sinopec and Petrochina, China's largest oil companies and biggest service station owners, led the opposition and a struggle between market forces and monopolistic power, between fuel choice and petropoly, ensued. The pushback, mostly having to do with oil majors' concerns about reduced profitability, threw sand into the gears, and the central government's enthusiasm for methanol cooled down.[4] Like in the United States, in China, provincial governments - the equivalent to America's state governments - sometimes take the lead where the nation's capital fails to act. Fully committed to methanol, the Shanxi government fought back, threatening to offer sales rights for methanol fuel directly to local independent stations, and eventually succeeded in convincing Sinopec and its allies to sell methanol blends in their properties in large scale and without price discrimination.

With methanol penetrating the stations, China's automakers began to certify their cars to run on the fuel and even produced dedicated cars that could run on it. These include Chery Automobile, the country's fastest growing independent automaker, which makes methanol FFVs, Shanghai Automotive Industry Corporation, Shanghai Maple Automobile which makes 60,000 M100 cars per year, Geely Automotive, Chang'an, Huapa Automotive, FAW and Jingye Company.[5] Methanol's low cost is particularly attractive to high mileage drivers like taxi owners. And indeed a burgeoning industry of retrofitting taxis to run on M85 and M100 developed, and with retrofit capacity of 30,000 cars per year this industry ensured that by 2012 79,000 taxis in Shanxi regularly fueled with methanol.[6] Taxi drivers are now reporting an annual fuel savings of 10,000-30,000 Yuan ($1,500-$5,000.)[7] The unsubsidized cost of taxi conversions to methanol would be 5000 Yuan, paid for with fuel savings in two to six months of driving. As unnecessary icing on the cake, taxi retrofits are subsidized by Shanxi provincial government to the tune of 1000 Yuan, or 20 percent of cost, while bus conversions are subsidized with 5000 Yuan, or 50 percent of cost.

M15 Fuel Station in Taiyuan

The future of China's methanol program

As the world economy wobbles, all eyes are turned to China. Where China goeth so goes the global economy. Many believe that China too is facing an economic crisis. Bad banks, inefficient state-owned enterprises, corruption and a real estate bubble have been mentioned as factors that might cause the Chinese economy to hit a nasty speed bump. But despite the warnings and the weakness in some of China's leading export markets, the Middle Kingdom has been able to demonstrate a remarkably impressive growth rate of nearly 10 percent per year. To be sure, China will slow down, but for an economy comprising a fifth of humanity, even a five percent growth rate instead of ten is non-trivial. China's growth will continue to set the tone in global energy markets and its appetite for oil will continue to be one of the major drivers affecting international energy security. Like the United States, China is heavily dependent on foreign oil, but while America's demand is approaching its peak, China's oil imports, currently at 60 percent of consumption, are heading nowhere but north. Behind this growth is the size and growth rate of the Chinese automobile market, already the world's largest. Consider this: in 1998 there were nine cars in China for every 1,000 people. Today there are more than 50 vehicles for every 1,000 people in China, compared to 800 vehicles per 1,000 people in the United States and 600 cars per 1,000 people in the EU. The market for cars in China is expected to grow by 12 percent a year in the next several years, rising from 18 million car sales per year in 2012 to 21 million by 2015 and 30 million by 2020. This market is the most vibrant in the world. According to J.D. Power and Associates, in 2012 Chinese enjoyed the world's widest range of new vehicles, with 94 brands and 476 models from which to choose. Compare this with fewer than 40 brands and nearly 100 fewer models available in the U.S. market, the second-largest automotive market in the world in 2011.[8] Eight out of 10 new car buyers in China are purchasing a vehicle for the first time in their lives, and only one in 10 new car buyers relies on car loans to fund their purchase. In other words, there is plenty of cash for new cars. With such growth China is projected to reach 300 cars per 1,000 people or 450 million vehicles by 2050.[9] China's methanol industry has a rosy future.

One good reason for this is that with the world's largest reserve of technically recoverable shale gas, China is likely to follow the footsteps of the United States and substantially increase its domestic natural gas production. In fact, in 2009 during President Obama's visit to Beijing, the United

States and China formed the U.S.-China Shale Gas Resource Initiative with the intent of speeding this process along. This will enable China to augment its methanol industry with natural gas derived alcohol. Assuming China continues its pursuit of methanol blending it will not take long before most of the cars sold there are made to run on methanol, in addition to or instead of gasoline. We asked GM's China representatives how the company will respond to the market's tilt toward methanol. Admitting their concern about the potential impact of M15 use in older vehicles, they acknowledged that GM's newer products are already robust enough to handle the fuel and that should China decide to adopt a national standard for methanol blends GM could easily – and willingly – respond to the challenge. Surely GM would not give up on its largest market, one that already buys two million of its cars annually. Let's hope that this quintessential American company then gives us the same choice in fuels it provides the Chinese.

What can America learn from China's experience?

Methanol works. To paraphrase Billy Rose's song: Fifty million Chinese can't be wrong. China's grand experiment provides the United States with an opportunity to observe, learn and build on. And there are some important lessons to absorb. First, what is clear from China's experience is that our existing cars and trucks *can* run on at least 15 percent methanol, perhaps even more, without any impact on the engine. Cars that drove on methanol over a long period of time were examined by Chinese and Western experts and no evidence of corrosive impact on the vehicle engine could be found. Nor was there any increase in the workload of auto mechanics or any malfunctions that required recalls. The fact that our cars are not warrantied to run on the fuel doesn't mean they can't. The automakers' excuses and snubs fall flat on their faces once the rubber met Taiyuan's roads. Second, claims of safety issues and other red flags raised by methanol detractors regarding its toxicity and corrosiveness are red herrings. After years of widespread use, with over 100 million refuelings with methanol, no health problems have been registered among the thousands of workers who deal with the fuel on a daily basis and certainly not among the millions of motorists fueling their cars. Third, the use of methanol has resulted in significant betterment of air quality. Shanxi officials reported a 20 percent decrease in harmful emissions like carbon monoxide (CO) and nitrogen oxide (NOx) and a 70 percent decrease in particulate matter – the soot and dust particles in the air that enter our body and park in our lungs. The use of methanol in high blends did show a slight increase in formaldehyde which is a human carcinogen. (When the Beijing Institute of Technology ran tests on formaldehyde emissions from a low methanol blend - M15 - in 2011, the emissions were lower than those of gasoline.) But the benzene which is added to our gasoline today to boost octane is carcinogenic as well so this is a wash, there's no obvious increased risk with methanol. Fourth, China's experience provides us with a better approximation of methanol's mileage. As mentioned before methanol packs half as much energy per gallon as gasoline but it is higher octane, and improvement in an engine's compression ratio offsets some of the range loss. Cars in China across dozens of models report a methanol to gasoline miles per gallon ratio of 1:1.6 – that is, per unit volume methanol goes 62.5 percent the distance of the same volume of gasoline. Fifth, methanol is significantly cheaper than gasoline. In May 2012, the price of M100 was 2.8 yuan/liter; the price of regular gasoline was 8.30 yuan/liter. M100 price was therefore 34 percent that of gasoline per liter. Since a liter of methanol will take you 62.5 percent as far as a liter of gasoline, that means the cost per mile of methanol is about half that of gasoline, a substantial savings. With such price disparity, no wonder illegal blending is so rampant in China. Sixth, and most important, is the role of government. The success of methanol deployment in China happened *despite* the national government, not because of it, and was driven by market forces. For the most part, the central government's attitude toward methanol was inconsistent and sporadic due to bureaucratic changes, political pressures from the national oil industry and a schizophrenic attitude toward greenhouse gas emissions. Coal-derived methanol emits about twice as much greenhouse gas as gasoline on a lifecycle basis. So whenever the central government decided to adopt greenhouse gas-curbing policies, support for methanol waned. At the sub-national level, the situation was very different. Less exposed to international pressure to reduce greenhouse gas emissions, provincial governments think more local than global and are more interested in addressing immediate pollution problems than the overall health of the planet. Local air quality is a much greater concern to them than greenhouse gas. Therefore, they could stay the course, providing guidance and certainty, establishing standards and creating ad-hoc solutions to the pressing issues surrounding methanol adoption. In the United States, where methanol is likely to be made from natural gas and biomass rather than coal, this tradeoff shouldn't exist as both natural gas and biomass derived methanol emit less greenhouse gas than gasoline. Furthermore, methanol derived from U.S. natural gas would be cheaper than Chinese coal-derived methanol. In terms of resource base, cheap natural gas and technical knowhow, no other country in the world is as well-equipped as the United States to open its vehicles – and thus its transportation fuel market - to methanol in large quantities. Will we have the will to do so?

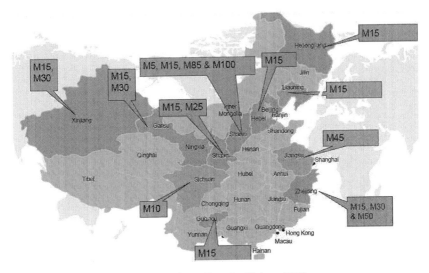

Methanol blending in China, 2012

7
THE FUEL WE LOVE TO HATE

*Ethanol is one of the most shameless energy rackets
going, in a field with no shortage of competitors.*
Wall Street Journal Editorial, March 16, 2009

Ethanol has been for decades at the center of a huge political controversy. Most politically aware people have strong opinions about it. Sometime it seems America is divided into two camps: ethanol lovers and ethanol haters. Over the years, both camps have clashed over the merit of the fuel, its energy balance and efficiency, its environmental qualities, and its impact on food prices. Each one of those became a topic of hot debate in which each side hurled its commissioned studies, expert opinions, recruited pundits and congressional champions. What provoked such intense anti-ethanol sentiment which brought respected newspapers like the *Wall Street Journal* and *Time Magazine* to refer to it as "scam," "fraud," "racket," and "boondoggle" - or the usually on target business commentator Larry Kudlow to ludicrously blame ethanol for the political upheaval in Egypt - were not the physical properties of this domestically produced fuel nor its much contested energy-in-energy-out balance, a nonsensical metric if there ever was one.[1] After all, there are many products we consume whose energy balance is far worse; as food expert Michael Pollan noted, it takes 10 calories of fossil-fuel energy to produce a single calorie of modern supermarket food. We still eat three meals per day plus snacks, but none of them have been attacked as venomously as ethanol.[2] Has anybody seen a study or heard a pundit complaining about the energy balance of gasoline? It's not great. Think how much energy is needed to produce the gasoline we pour into our tanks. Pumping seawater into the wells in Saudi Arabia to increase reservoir pressure, pumping the oil out of the well, transporting the crude to processing facilities where sulfur and other impurities are removed, loading the oil on a tanker, powering the tanker on a one-month voyage across two oceans, refining the oil into gasoline (ten percent of crude's energy is lost right there) and distributing the gasoline to gas stations throughout the country all require energy. A lot of it. More than ethanol. The amount of fossil fuel in mega joules needed to make one mega joule of gasoline is 1.19 versus 0.77 for corn ethanol and 0.10 for cellulosic ethanol.[3] The point is: gasoline's energy requirement is greater than ethanol's (unless we count the energy of the sun absorbed by corn plants, which would be a pretty odd thing to do given that the sun doesn't charge us) and yet this hasn't prevented any of us from using this "net energy loser."[4] The fact is, the market just doesn't care about energy return on energy invested, aka Eroei. As Peter Huber has eloquently written:

> Eroei calculations now litter the energy policy debate. Time and again they're wheeled out to explain why one form of energy just can't win - tar sands, shale, corn, wood, wind, you name it. Even quite serious journals--*Science*, for example--have published pieces along these lines. [...] In the real world, however, investors don't care a fig whether they earn positive Eroei. What they care about is dollar return on dollar invested. And the two aren't the same--nowhere close--because different forms of energy command wildly different prices. Invest ten units of 10-cent energy to capture one unit of $10 energy and you lose energy but gain dollars, and Wall Street will fund you from here to Alberta.[5]

So what's going on here? The truth is that the debate about ethanol is not about what ethanol is or about its fuel properties but mainly about what it represents to us. The spectacle of presidential wannabes kowtowing to ethanol producers in Des Moines in order to get their support in the Iowa caucuses (though with much less enthusiasm in the 2012 election cycle), the direct and indirect agricultural subsidies for the ethanol industry, many of them vestiges of the bygone era of the Great Depression, the federal mandate to use it and the scandalous tariff on imported ethanol (finally eliminated in December 2011) all symbolize what most of us dislike about Washington: undue government intervention in the free market, abuse of taxpayers' dollars, political favoritism and growing K Street influence over our government. What sparked the ire of ethanol opponents more than anything was the $6 billion a year de facto cash subsidy in the form of Volumetric Ethanol Excise Tax Credit (VEETC) that directed 45 cents to refiners for every gallon of ethanol they blended with gasoline. The direct beneficiaries of the notorious ethanol subsidies were not the farmers or even the Archer Daniels Midlands or Cargills of the world but rather the big oil and refining companies such as Valero, ConocoPhillips, ExxonMobil, and BP. The latter alone raked in approximately $600 million in VEETC in the very same year its blown out deepwater Horizon well spilled millions of barrels of oil into the Gulf of Mexico.[6] But with the new atmosphere of fiscal tightness, VEETC was one of the first government programs to be placed on the chopping block and was effectively terminated in December 2011 along with the 54 cents per gallon import tariff on Brazilian ethanol. Now when the two notorious protectionist measures are no more, ethanol opponents have only one branch left to hang on.

The Energy Policy Act of 2005 included a Renewable Fuel Standard (RFS1), which mandated that as of 2006 a minimum amount of renewable fuels - 4 billion gallons - be blended by refiners into gasoline prior to distribution. This requirement increased to 7.5 billion gallons by 2012 (equivalent to about 5 percent of total gasoline consumed), and in 2007 the Energy Independence and Security Act of 2007 (EISA) revised RFS1 and greatly expanded the mandate to 36 billion gallons (equivalent to about 11 percent of total gasoline consumed) of renewable fuels by 2022 (RFS2). The rationale for the expansion: a Soviet central planning style carving out of market share for cellulosic ethanol, a pet project of the G.W. Bush administration and the then-Congress. The criticism of the RFS is not unjustified. When a group of bureaucrats dictates how much of a certain product should be in the market at any given year that just does not bode well with free marketers. Which is why even post-VEETC, fiscal conservatives are still not prepared to show goodwill toward ethanol. On the other side is the ethanol industry, protesting that since the cars and distribution system are blocked to competition absent the RFS it couldn't otherwise grow a market. Both sides have a point. But policies that smack of favoritism give fodder to ethanol detractors. The result: despite the fact that on a gasoline equivalent basis, ethanol's contribution to the U.S. fuel market is second only to that of Canada, the top oil supplier to the U.S., many Americans identify the fuel with pork and corruption rather than with energy security. Our view? We can't abide "four legs good, two legs bad" thinking. Criticize the policy, but don't tar the fuel qua fuel with it. Evaluate the fuel on its own merits, with the chief metric being how it stacks up on the economics against gasoline.

Is ethanol an economic loser?

Let us be clear. We are opposed to agricultural subsidies of any kind. For corn, for sugar, for soybeans, for anything. U.S. agricultural policy is a sham. We pay farmers not to farm, and we have unwarranted tariffs, quotas and trade barriers on imported products. These are all bad, market skewing policies. Those up in arms about earmarks would do well to understand the pat my back and I'll pat yours problem extends much further than that in our political system. Take a look at the U.S. tariff schedule which carves out protected niches for everything from screws to sun umbrellas. Talk about government spreading favors. In any case, ethanol is not a perfect fuel. Far from it. Like methanol, it packs less energy per gallon than gasoline, it depends on the volatile agricultural sector and, like other alcohols, is more corrosive than gasoline. But as we all know, petroleum is not free of problems either, and our oil dependence is costing us more and more every year. Which is why our judgment on ethanol should be based on two questions: can ethanol be cost competitive with gasoline, and are its external security and economic costs lower than those of gasoline? The answer to the first question is, it depends on the price of oil, and the answer to the second question is yes.

From an economic standpoint, the main point to consider is that ethanol is a domestic fuel, and those profiting from it are hardworking, tax paying Americans who plow most of their earnings back into the U.S. economy. Comprised of approximately 200 plants in 26 states with nameplate capacity of roughly 14 billion gallons per year, the economic activities of the ethanol industry put $36 billion into the pockets of Americans in 2010. The full impact of the spending for annual operations, construction of new capacity and R&D is estimated to have supported $53.6 billion of the nation's GDP.[7] In the process, the ethanol industry helped create more than 400,000 full and part time jobs. None of this can be said about foreign oil. When we import oil we pump money into the economies of some of the worst regimes in the world, and most of that money is never recycled back into our economy. Those rooting for the demise of the ethanol industry should grapple with a hard truth: Between 2005 and 2012, the years in which U.S. import dependency dropped from 60 to 42 percent, ethanol was the largest single component in volumetric terms of America's domestic liquid fuel supply growth, more than domestic drilling. It has also had more of an impact on oil displacement than the increase in average vehicle fuel efficiency.[8]

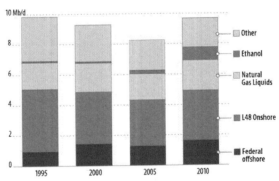

Domestic oil and other liquid fuel supply in million b/d

Source: Congressional Research Service

They should also stop and think what would have happened to the U.S. economy if ethanol did not exist. Today, ethanol comprises about 10 percent of the fuel that goes into our tanks. Without these 14 billion gallons, an extra 485 million barrels of oil would have had to be imported in 2011 to fill the gap, roughly equivalent to 13 percent of total U.S. crude oil imports. This amounts to $50 billion dollars that ethanol saved the U.S. economy. According to Merrill Lynch, by adding supply to the fuel market and thus taking off some of the pressure at the height of oil prices in the summer of 2008, ethanol was responsible for keeping the price of oil 15 percent lower than where it would have otherwise been.[9] Irritating as the VEETC was, it saved Americans much more money than it actually cost. From January 2000 to December 2011, the U.S. ethanol industry produced 74 billion gallons. During this period, blenders received $30 billion in VEETC. On the other side of the ledger, over the same period of time the growth in ethanol production reduced wholesale gasoline prices by $0.29 per gallon on average.[10] This means that if not for ethanol, American consumers would have paid an extra $300 billion over that decade. In other words, the ethanol program saved taxpayers ten times the amount it actually cost them. No matter where one stands on ethanol, from a purely economic perspective, even a bad policy like the VEETC was not such a bad deal.

The food vs. fuel myth

But what about ethanol's impact on our food purchases? One of the most widely touted anti-ethanol claims is that the U.S. corn ethanol effort is affecting food production around the world – America included – and even starving poor people. Reports to that effect began to inundate the media when oil prices were at their 2008 peak, causing a public relations disaster to the biofuels industry. It seemed so obvious, the headlines blared, that with so much corn being turned into fuel, food shortages must inevitably result, and so if there are bread riots in Egypt or tortilla riots in Mexico, it must be because of America, its profligate motorists and its corn ethanol program, not because of the corrupt and incompetent regimes that steal billions from their people. Contrary explanations for the rise in food prices, including the rise in oil prices, the role of commodity markets and the fact that hundreds of millions of people in China and India are rising out of poverty and moving from mere subsistence to a more calorie rich diet and hence demanding more meat which put pressure on the grain market (it takes eighteen calories of grain to produce one calorie of meat) were ignored by the pundits who eagerly jumped on the anti-ethanol bandwagon. Anti-ethanol statements coming from America's reporters and pundits were music to the ears of some of America's critics abroad. A U.N. special rapporteur on the right to food, Jean Ziegler, called biofuels a "crime against humanity;"[11] Cuban leader Fidel Castro called the Bush administration's ethanol project "genocidal", and his protégé, Venezuela's Hugo Chavez, referred to it as "true madness."[12] Unsurprisingly, the Islamists have also put ethanol in their sights. Mohammed al-Najimi, a prominent scholar at the Saudi Islamic Jurisprudence Academy, warned students traveling outside Saudi Arabia not to drive any vehicles powered with ethanol "because the prophet has cursed not only who drinks it but also those who use it for other purposes."[13] The Saudi Oil Minister Ali al-Naimi, the man who effectively runs OPEC, repeatedly resorts to the old scare tactics every time oil importing nations declare their intention to promote competitors to oil. In 2009, he warned that such efforts could have a "chilling effect" on investment in the oil sector and that "a nightmare scenario would be created if alternative energy supplies fail to meet overly optimistic expectations, while traditional energy suppliers scale back investment."[14] Translation: if you keep investing in fuels like ethanol, we are going to cut back on investment in oil to make sure oil prices stay high. OPEC went even further in denigrating competing fuels by highlighting their downsides. Through its Fund for International Development (OFID), OPEC commissioned an anti-biofuels study which highlighted all the reasons biofuels should be discouraged.[15] Not surprisingly, the conclusion of the study was that an "accelerated growth of biofuels production is threatening the availability of adequate food supplies for humans, by diverting land, water and other resources away from food and feed crops." The Fund's director, Suleiman Jasir Al-Herbish, explained in his introduction to the study that "OFID seeks to uphold its time-honored tradition of promoting debate on issues of special interest to developing countries." How ironic it is that the cartel that for decades impoverished the world's poor through longstanding restrictive production policies was among the first to warn the developing world against the supposed dangers of biofuels. Astonishingly, ethanol was even blamed for driving up the price of oil. OPEC's president alleged that 40 percent of the rise in oil prices can be attributed to the – note the word - "intrusion" of ethanol.[16] In the summer of 2008, as oil price hit peak after peak, ethanol, the only competitor that was somewhat able to keep the lid on gasoline prices, was facing the most ferocious attack ever.

Contrary to popular thinking, it was not "Big Oil," and not even OPEC, that initiated the food vs fuel tale but rather the Grocery Manufacturers Association (GMA), the trade group representing scores of processed food manufacturers like Kraft Foods, Nestle and Pepsi. In order to understand the snack makers' interest in bashing ethanol one needs to understand America's sugar policy. The United States has sugar quotas that keep American sugar prices artificially high above world prices – kept in place by a sugar lobby that gives equal opportunity campaign contributions to both Democrats and Republicans – and at the same time, for years, federal agricultural policy kept corn prices artificially low through a price support system that disconnected corn price from actual demand. So while around the world sugar is used to sweeten baked goods, cereals, and soft drinks, in the United States, food manufacturers became accustomed to using cheap – taxpayer subsidized – corn syrup. Just pick up a bottle of ketchup or a can of Coke in the United States and then one in Europe or Asia and compare the ingredients. The sugar lobby is formidable: check out which politicians receive its donations and then see how they vote on abolishing the sugar tariff. In 2007, as oil prices began to skyrocket, demand for ethanol, an available competitor to gasoline, was growing by leaps and bounds. After realizing that this new use for corn was threatening to bite into their profit margins by moving the price of corn to an economically sustainable footing - that is, one where corn farmers were no longer receiving price supports - the GMA, also known as the junk food lobby, decided to launch an aggressive PR campaign in an effort to roll back the 2007 ethanol mandates that passed in the previous year's energy bill. (We'll pause here to note that we don't support those mandates for free market reasons, but disliking a policy is quite a different thing from making ludicrous claims about the fuel that policy is focused on.) In March 2008, GMA began searching for a PR firm to help it build "a global center-left coalition" against ethanol and hire "trusted third-party experts" who would link ethanol to global hunger and poverty. (Interestingly, around the same time, some natural gas companies funded a similar center-left coalition effort against coal use for electricity generation, spreading money to environmental groups like the Sierra Club to demonize the competing commodity. But the shale gas revolution and environmentalists worries over fracking eventually caused a messy divorce in that partnership.) A competent Washington PR firm, Glover Park, won the anti-ethanol account and the campaign to obliterate ethanol was under way.[17] It proved to be one of the most successful de-branding efforts since the anti-cigarettes campaign. The campaign united existing anti-ethanol forces and media outlets into an effective coalition, and the unprepared ethanol industry was caught by surprise, like a deer in the headlights.

Then came the financial meltdown of 2009 which proved that the food vs. fuel claim was a farce. The crisis revealed that food commodity prices track oil prices regardless of how much corn is used for ethanol production. When oil was up, it affected the cost of essential components of our food supply chain like fertilizers and transportation. When oil prices crashed, food commodity prices quickly followed. Between July and November 2008, oil fell nearly 50 percent. In the same period of time, corn prices fell by the exact same figure. Was this because we used less ethanol? No. To the contrary, ethanol production capacity increased substantially from 9 billion gallons in 2008 to nearly 11 billion gallons in 2009. Production capacity continued to grow to 13.2 billion gallons in 2010 reaching 14 billion gallons in 2011.[18] As the numbers in Table 7.1 show, there is no correlation between U.S. ethanol production and the price of corn. Ethanol production has been on a steady increase while corn prices have fluctuated in perfect correlation with global commodity prices.

Table 7.1: US Ethanol Production versus Corn Prices

Year	Average Corn price ($/bushel)	U.S. Ethanol production (Billion gallons/y)
2007	$4.00	6.5
2008	$7.50	9.0
2009	$3.50	10.6
2010	$3.50	13.2
2011	$6.50	14.2

The reality was that grain prices were driven up by the same wave that jacked up the price of copper, rice and coffee beans. When the commodity bubble popped, prices declined. This is not to say that ethanol had no impact at all on food prices. It did. But this impact was marginal in comparison to the other factors in play. A 2009 study by the Congressional Budget Office (CBO) found that in the period between

April 2007 and April 2008, food costs as measured by the consumer price index went up 5.1 percent. Higher corn prices accounted for 0.5 to 0.8 percentage points of the increase. In other words increased corn ethanol production accounted for only 10 to 15 percent of total increased food costs. "Over the same period, certain other factors – for example, higher energy costs – had a greater effect on food prices than did use of ethanol as a motor fuel," the CBO determined.[19] In other words, 90 percent of the rise in food prices had nothing to do with ethanol. The World Bank, which prior to the financial crisis blamed biofuels for driving up prices, retracted its position in a July 2010 report titled *Placing the 2006/08 Commodity Price Boom into Perspective*, concluding that the effect of biofuels on food prices has not been as large as originally thought, but that the use of commodities by financial investors may have been partly responsible for the spike. The report said:

> Worldwide, biofuels account for only about 1.5 percent of the area under grains/oilseeds. This raises serious doubts about claims that biofuels account for a big shift in global demand. Even though widespread perceptions about such a shift played a big role during the recent commodity price boom, it is striking that maize prices hardly moved during the first period of increase in U.S. ethanol production, and oilseed prices dropped when the EU increased impressively its use of biodiesel.[20]

The reason ethanol's impact on manufactured food prices was so minimal was because the cost of food ingredients in food products we buy at the supermarket represents on average only one fifth of the price at checkout. When it comes to corn, the cost of the ingredient is much lower. A $3.00 box of cornflakes contains 15 oz of corn. In 2008, the corn content of that box cost 8 cents when bought from the farmer. Farm commodity prices have a minor effect on the retail consumers. But the effect of oil price hikes can be huge – and not just on food, but on all consumer goods requiring fuel for processing or transport.

These arguments did not make an impression on the general public. In fact, the food vs. fuel controversy opened the door to a debate of the morality of using land and food crops for non-food uses. That millions of acres are used to grow cotton for clothing, fire wood, flowers, Christmas trees, and let's not forget, plenty of alcohol in the form of beer, wine, and hard liquor, was not enough of a reason to spark a debate about "food vs. clothes," "food vs. flowers," or "food vs. booze." It was food vs. fuel that caught all the attention. But who is to determine what is the most moral use of any commodity? Is feeding a child corn syrup rich Coke and a corn syrup loaded Twinkie, hence increasing his or her chances of suffering from obesity and juvenile diabetes, more moral than driving him or her to school on corn rich ethanol fuel? Who decides? Both the GMA and OPEC prefer the former choice. How about you?

What's next for ethanol?

Sad but true, despite its economic merits and its undeniable contribution to our energy security, ethanol is today a tarnished brand. Just like the electric vehicle, it has become another victim of identity politics. In the era of the Tea Party, which is rightly focused on the ever burgeoning size and intrusiveness of our government, and at a time of budgetary tightness, it is unfortunate that ethanol bashing is another litmus test which one must pass to win fiscal conservative credentials. It is amazing what a difference four years have made. In the 2008 election cycle, all of the Republican presidential candidates were unequivocally pro-ethanol, at least until Iowa. Even Senator John McCain, one of the harshest ethanol critics in the Senate, got softer on ethanol, proclaiming himself a "strong" supporter. "I support ethanol and I think it is a vital, a vital alternative energy source not only because of our dependency on foreign oil but its greenhouse gas reduction effects," the Straight Talk Express uttered.[21] But in the 2012 cycle, none of Republican candidates had one good word to say about ethanol, not on their websites, not on the stump, not even in Iowa. It was the one competitor to oil no one wanted to touch. Tim Pawlenty, the former Governor of Minnesota, one of the nation's largest ethanol producing and consuming states, chose to kick off his campaign for the Republican presidential nomination in corn kingdom Iowa, deriding ethanol subsidies. Former House Speaker Newt Gingrich, who between 2009 and early 2011 was a paid consultant to a major ethanol advocacy group called Growth Energy, earning more than $575,000, and who publicly proclaimed ethanol was "pro-American" because of its potential to reduce the nation's reliance on foreign oil, avoided the E word like a ghost during his campaign.[22] On Capitol Hill, it was sadly par for the course that some of the same politicians who railed most loudly against ethanol were all-in when it came to supporting massive subsidies for CNG vehicles. Talk about hypocrisy.

It was not only the political Right that abandoned ethanol. The Left, which on all things related to energy defers to the environmental movement, has too distanced itself from the fuel. The most visible turnabout was made by Mr. Environment, former Vice President Al Gore, who in

November 2012 confessed: "One of the reasons I made that mistake [of supporting ethanol] is that I paid particular attention to the farmers in my home state of Tennessee, and I had a certain fondness for the farmers in the state of Iowa because I was about to run for president."[23] Ethanol began to lose its allure with environmentalists when studies popped up claiming that ethanol causes more greenhouse gas to be emitted than the gasoline it replaces if *indirect* carbon dioxide emissions are taken into account. Indirect analysis counts the carbon dioxide released when farmers in the developing world supposedly plow and burn forests or grassland to grow energy crops used to make biofuels or to grow food to replace previously imported food crops whose supply was reduced by the demand for ethanol. Particularly influential among those was a *Science Magazine* article by Timothy Searchinger, formerly staff attorney at an environmental organization, in which he argued that United States ethanol production is driving agriculture to expand in the developing world, a process that according to him in significant part entails burning down forests and plowing up grasslands, thus releasing twice as much carbon dioxide to the air as the original amount of displaced gasoline would.[24]

First, Searchinger's method and the whole school of indirect carbon dioxide analysis relies on deeply flawed thinking. As Robert Zubrin puts it, "using indirect analysis, it is possible to show that *any* technology or policy which can be plausibly argued to confer any social benefit whatsoever will cause global warming. For example, both *tax cuts* (because they give consumers greater spending power) and *tax increases* (because they allow for expanded funding of health care and public education, which in turn contribute to longer lifespans and income growth) can be considered indirect causes of global warming. [...] the U.S. corn ethanol program is [thus viewed as] contemptible because it (allegedly) opens up market opportunities for Third World peasants—which is to say, precisely because of the humanitarian good it would do by lifting them from poverty."[25] Secondly, the deforestation argument is bunk. While the problem exists in the case of Indonesia, which cleared forests and planted in their stead palm plantations for biodiesel, it does not exist in the case of ethanol, and certainly not in Brazil. Deforestation in Brazil is primarily caused by timber production and cattle ranching so the cutting down of the Amazon rainforest has to do with our steaks, furniture, newspapers, books, and the 24 rolls of extra-soft bathroom tissue most of us flush down each year - not ethanol. The Amazon's climate is not even suitable for growing sugar cane. As one can clearly see in the map below

Brazil's sugar plantations are as far away from the Amazon as Texas is from Nicaragua.

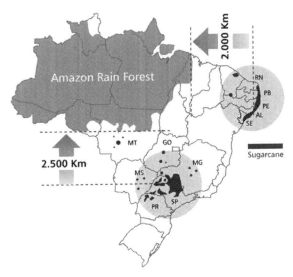

Brazil's sugar plantations: nowhere near the rain forests

Source: UNICA

Buying into the land-use changes doctrine, the California Air Resources Board (CARB), the same agency that in 2003 gained notoriety for its role in "killing" the electric car, included in its Low Carbon Fuel Standard provisions requiring that the entire life cycle carbon footprint be considered – that means indirect effects as well. This decision essentially killed the use of Midwest ethanol in California. According to CARB's calculations, Midwest ethanol releases 75 grams of carbon dioxide equivalent per megajoule of energy produced. Gasoline releases 95. In other words, ethanol beats gasoline. However, if land-use changes are included, ethanol jumps to 105 while gasoline remains 95. Now gasoline beats ethanol. More infuriating was the fact that CARB's calculations for gasoline applied only to California oil when almost 60 percent of the state's oil use is imported, mostly from Alaska, Saudi Arabia, Iraq and Ecuador. In this CARB failed to apply similar accounting for indirect greenhouse gas emissions for foreign oil such as the military operations related to defending our access to oil. After all, the jets, tanks, ships and Humvees patrolling the Persian Gulf or the Special Forces protecting oil facilities worldwide don't run on vegetable oil, and the electricity powering military bases dedicated to protecting our access to oil is not made on wind farms. Ignoring those while speculating about the role of deforestation is selective bias, not science. Michael Wang from the Center for Transportation Research at the Argonne National Laboratory who applied a vastly different and more realistic methodology found that on a per gallon basis, when the full "life cycle" of the fuel, from growing the feedstock (or recovering it from the ground in the case of oil) to producing the fuel and burning it, is taken into account, corn ethanol reduces greenhouse gas emissions by 18 percent to 29 percent compared with gasoline, sugarcane ethanol reduces emissions by 56 percent and cellulosic ethanol has an even greater benefit with more than 80 percent reduction.[26] Another report commissioned by the International Energy Agency (IEA) examined greenhouse gas reductions from grain ethanol since 1995 and concluded that thanks to improvements in both feedstock production and ethanol production, greenhouse gas reductions have grown from approximately 26 percent in 1995 to over 39 percent today, while projected greenhouse gas reductions from ethanol will reach nearly 55 percent in 2015.[27]

The CARB ruling had another ramification. Because it declared Midwest ethanol as supposedly more carbon intensive vis-à-vis gasoline it skewed the market in favor of Brazilian ethanol which is made from sugar cane. This type of ethanol emits 27 grams of carbon dioxide over its lifecycle and, with land-use factored in, 73 grams which is still lower than gasoline. The real world implications of the policy were absurd: California, the largest ethanol-consuming state outside of the Midwest, imported sugarcane ethanol from Brazil rather than corn ethanol from the Midwest. In turn, corn ethanol from the Midwest was shipped to the Gulf of Mexico by rail and then to Brazil via tankers to replace the volume Brazil sent to the United States. This environmental shell game resulted in the economic waste (not to mention extra added emissions) of unnecessarily burning a gigantic amount of marine fuel in the process of shipping corn ethanol 6,200 miles from Houston to Brazil while a roughly equal amount of sugarcane ethanol travels 8,400 miles in the opposite direction from Brazil to California. Luckily, in December 2011 a sound minded federal judge put an end to the fiasco – at least for now – granting a preliminary injunction against the implementation of California's Low Carbon Fuel Standard. Rejecting CARB's appeal, he concluded that the regulation: "impermissibly treads into the province and powers of our federal government, reaching beyond its boundaries to regulate activity wholly outside of its borders."[28]

Fixing the brand

All of the facts and arguments in defense of ethanol may be true, but in the court of public opinion ethanol lost the battle for the hearts and minds of large portions of the American public on both the Right and the Left. As a *Wall Street Journal* editorial once summed up the situation: "Everyone hates ethanol."[29]

Can there be a resurrection? This would depend more than anything on the conduct of the ethanol industry itself. This fractured industry, represented by several competing organizations including the Renewable Fuels Association, Growth Energy, American Coalition for Ethanol and the Clean Fuels Development Coalition, is at a critical junction in its history. Ignoring the image crisis it faces and hedging its bets on a dwindling group of ethanol champions in Congress would bring more of the same and under certain circumstances drive the industry's decline. On the other hand, embarking on a fresh strategy could quickly shift the political landscape in favor of the embattled fuel. In order to better understand the choices the industry is facing, one must understand its mode of operation thus far.

For decades, the American ethanol industry focused on two goals: growth and protectionism. Between 2007 and 2012 the industry more than doubled its production. Ethanol yield per bushel of corn in the United States has increased significantly since 1980 and is likely to continue to do so in the years to come. This is partly due to the increase in corn yield per acre – in 2007, corn growers produced on average 151 bushels per acre (according to the ethanol industry, this number is projected to grow to 211 by 2018) and partly due to improvement in refining techniques. What gave the industry its impressive boost was the designation of the octane booster MTBE as a carcinogenic groundwater pollutant. After MTBE was banned in 2005, ethanol became the only economically feasible fuel additive for states with air quality problems. The existence of the VEETC subsidy only made it more compelling for the refiners. Predictably, the demand for ethanol increased at unprecedented rates as most refiners replaced MTBE with ethanol. But as an oxygenator, ethanol could only be blended into gasoline at a ratio of up to 10 percent which meant that soon enough domestic production hit what is known as the blend wall. For vehicles to be able to use significantly higher percentages of alcohol, they need to be designated as fuel flexible. With spare production capacity for which there is no U.S. market ethanol producers are forced to export their product. Rather than focusing on opening vehicles and thus the fuel market to full competition, tearing down the blend wall altogether, the industry's response has been to fight for lifting the blend wall a little higher to 15 percent. It succeeded. In 2012, the Environmental Protection Agency approved the first applications to sell E15, although only for vehicles from model year 2001 and later.

But the focus on lifting the blend wall was a short sighted approach. At current growth rates, the new wall will be reached in several years. What then? A fight for E20? E25? This question is particularly relevant in light of the perhaps imminent emergence of cellulosic ethanol as alternative to corn ethanol. The technology is not yet at large scale commercial production, but it is slowly getting there. In Emmetsburg, Iowa, ethanol producer POET will in 2013 launch Project Liberty, a commercial demonstration plant that will produce 25 million gallons per year of cellulosic ethanol from corn crop residue through a biological process. POET claims that its production costs will be under $2 a gallon. If such projects succeed, not to mention if cellulosic methanol joins the fray, they could easily crowd out corn ethanol as the former enjoy both production tax credits and a carved market share as part of RFS2. Fighting for a government protected market share is not going to endear the industry to the eyes of most of the American public and its representatives. More so, it is not conducive to positioning ethanol as a viable competitor to gasoline over market share and hence over price. Crawling forward and trying to squeeze a few more percentage points in the blend every several years is a shortsighted strategy which ensures that ethanol remains a big fish in a small pond. In other words, an additive, not a competitive fuel. On the other hand, fighting to ensure that vehicles and fuel distribution systems are open to using ethanol at any blend consumers desire would remove the blend wall forever, allowing ethanol, as well as other fuels, to combat gasoline at any pump, at any level and on board any car. May the least costly fuel at any given time win.

Needed: An American Alcohol Alliance

The challenge for ethanol today is mostly political. Support for the fuel comes primarily from Midwestern corn growers and ethanol producers. This political support base is concentrated in eight states with significant production capacity (over half a billion gallons per year): Iowa, Nebraska, Illinois, Minnesota, South Dakota, Indiana, Wisconsin and Kansas. In Washington's new political landscape, the ethanol block is not powerful enough compared to the seven-state oil block: Alaska, California, Texas, North Dakota, Oklahoma, and Wyoming, together supplying most of our onshore domestic crude plus Louisiana, America's refining hub. What is needed is a new non-subsidy pushing political alliance in support of alcohol fuels, one in which ethanol interests are only one of several stakeholders and one to which politicians from outside the Corn Belt can connect. We call it the American Alcohol Alliance (AAA). This alliance includes all the states with a resource base significant enough to potentially contribute to America's alcohol market. For such an alliance to emerge the ethanol industry must embrace methanol as an ally rather than view it as a competitor over a limited market share. This would take a lot. For all the rhetoric about "energy independence," "made-in-America fuels," and the need for "domestic jobs," the protected ethanol industry has been far from welcoming to the odd cousin vying for a swath of fuel market. To traditional ethanol producers, methanol is a threat. It is cheaper, far more scalable and, does not have the (albeit undeserved by ethanol) food competitor stigma, and, most important, requires no subsidies and giveaways. No wonder some of the harshest responses we have heard about methanol have come from ethanol promoters.

This is a myopic view which ignores the profound political benefits methanol can provide the ethanol industry. The introduction of methanol into the transportation fuel market would increase the number of states that can become fuel producers from 15 which are currently responsible for producing almost all of America's domestic liquid fuel supply to 32. As Table 7.2 shows, methanol would open the door to 17 more states to join the fuels market including 11 additional natural gas and coal states and at least six more states – Washington, North Carolina, Georgia, Mississippi, Florida and Alabama – with a significant forest residue endowment. Entrepreneurs in each of those states would find in methanol an opportunity to leverage their natural resources by developing a local methanol industry. Put differently, methanol raises the number of potential alcohol states from eight to 32. Eight states have a local interest in the proliferation of ethanol. But three times as many states would have domestic interest in removing obstacles that prevent the proliferation of alcohol fuels writ large. That's one half of the United States Senate. For example: an important state like Pennsylvania has no local industry interest in ethanol. However, the state is rich in coal with a vast reserve of shale gas located at the Marcellus formation. With methanol in the game, Pennsylvania politicians will have a dog in the fight and they will be more likely to be supportive of policies that remove obstacles preventing alcohol fuels from competing against gasoline. Another example is Louisiana, an oil and natural gas hub and home to 16 refineries. The state has a significant natural gas endowment and two methanol plants under construction. With methanol in the mix, it too could be part of the AAA.

Table 7.2: Potential and actual fuel making states

	Coal Five billion tons +	Natural Gas Five trillion cubic feet+	Oil 500 million barrels +	Biomass 10,000 tons/year +
Alabama				X
Alaska	X	X	X	
Arizona				
Arkansas		X		X
California		X	X	X
Colorado	X	X		
Connecticut				
Delaware				
Florida				X
Georgia				X
Hawaii				
Idaho				
Illinois	X			X
Indiana	X			X
Iowa				X
Kansas				X
Kentucky	X			
Louisiana		X		X
Maine				
Maryland				
Massachusetts				
Michigan				X

Minnesota				X
Mississippi				X
Missouri	X			X
Montana	X			
Nebraska				X
Nevada				
New Hampshire				
New Jersey				
New Mexico	X	X		
New York				
North Carolina				X
North Dakota	X		X	X
Ohio	X			X
Oklahoma		X	X	
Oregon				
Pennsylvania	X	X		
Rhode Island				
South Carolina				
South Dakota				X
Tennessee				
Texas	X	X	X	X
Utah	X	X		
Vermont				
Virginia				
Washington				X
West Virginia	X	X		
Wisconsin				X
Wyoming	X	X	X	

It is perfectly understandable why the ethanol industry might view methanol with trepidation. While less energy dense, methanol is cheaper per unit energy. With the blend wall intact, any newcomer alcohol could elbow ethanol out of the market. When you're a big fish in a small pond, the last thing you want is to deal with a faster and more agile competitor. But should most new cars be fuel flexible, the blend wall thus eliminated and the market opened wide, there would be enough room for all alcohols to compete and thrive. After all, it costs more to make oil from tar sands in Canada than it does to lift a barrel in Saudi Arabia. So what? As long as the price of oil is higher than the Canadian production cost, tar sands can compete in the market. Only via a partnership with the methanol industry will ethanol makers be able to make their case. Will the ethanol industry keep fighting to eke out a few more percentage points of government protected market or will it support a more open and potentially lucrative free for all of a competitive fuel market? Time will tell. For now our judgment on ethanol is that it is a powerful, high octane fuel whose cost per mile as compared to gasoline is a function of the price of corn vs. the price of oil. None of the alleged problems associated with it warrant blocking it from competing in the fuel market. We have a strong bias against margarine. Rich in trans-fatty acids that are linked to coronary heart diseases, cancer and stroke, it is one of the unhealthiest foods we consume. It is also made from vegetable oils so we bet a brainy researcher could pen a study showing that just like some biofuels it too contributes to deforestation in Indonesia, food riots in Bangladesh or global warming. But are any of those claims enough to ban margarine from competing in the spreads market? Does anyone have the right to force us to consume only butter on the grounds that it is healthier? Were the pre-World War II federal and state governments right in appeasing the rent-seeking dairy lobbyists by passing laws to restrict the sale of margarine? A typical free marketer would say: put it on the shelf and let the consumer decide. In the same spirit, the deal we propose for ethanol is: open the fuel market so that no fuel is barred from competition - and let the market decide.

8
A PLATFORM FOR COMPETITION

A lot of times, people don't know what they want until you show it to them.
Steve Jobs, 1998

On January 9, 2007, the legendary Apple CEO Steve Jobs unveiled the iPhone. It was one of those sleek gadgets Jobs envisioned people did not think they needed until they got their hands on them or saw friends and relatives with them. His instinct proved right. Within six months, the iPhone hit the stores, creating international consumer hysteria. Over the first five quarters Apple sold 6.1 million iPhone units. Thereafter, sales grew steadily, and by mid-2012 more than 200 million iPhones were sold. Just 55 months after the unveiling of the device and with record revenues generated by its other successful products such as the iPad, iPod and iMac, Apple surpassed ExxonMobil as America's most valuable company by market capitalization. The iPhone was much more than just another successful gadget. It was a powerful innovation engine. In the same month that the iPhone hit stores, Apple announced that its platform would support third-party web applications soon to be known as "apps." Apple made available to third-party developers a free downloadable software development kit that allows them to develop iPhone apps and then test them in an "iPhone simulator." The developers can either release the application for free or set any price for it to be distributed through the App Store, of which they receive a 70 percent share. Once Apple provided the platform, it unleashed a tsunami of innovation. More than half a million apps have been developed, and by early 2011, the number of apps downloaded by Apple users reached an astounding 10 billion. The list of geeks, internet gold diggers and fame seekers who have stepped up to the plate with popular apps is growing by the day. The success stories about the 14-year old Utah boy who created the popular Bubble Boy puzzle game, the former Sun Microsystems engineer who quit his day job shortly after reportedly making more than $600,000 in only one month, or the "Heroes" TV star who launched a free app that distributes mobile coupons on behalf of hundreds of retailers have all inspired America's best and brightest to try their luck and talent developing apps of their own. Similar mobile operating systems like Google's Android have provided developers additional opportunities.

What does all this have to do with oil? The iPhone is a $400 platform that gave rise to a burgeoning industry of apps, making lots of people lots of money and in the process creating numerous new jobs (Steve Jobs' last name could not be more appropriate) and investment opportunities. Such low cost innovation and economic growth platforms are exactly what America needs today. Since the Great Recession began many jobs have been lost forever in part because we have become more efficient. A pizza parlor that employed fifteen workers before the Great Recession learned how to manage the workload with ten. It is not likely to rehire the five it let go even if the economy improves. While the resulting lower costs are great for the purchasers of the pizza and great for the parlor owners, they aren't so great for the people who used to have those jobs. The downside of increasing worker productivity is that the lag between the time GDP recovers and employment returns to the prerecession point is growing from recession to recession. It took three months for employment to bounce back to the pre-recession level after the 1973-74 recession. It took six months in 1981, fifteen months in 1990, and 39 months in 2001. The 2008 recession is likely to result in the longest jobless recovery, at least 60 months, perhaps much longer. According to a McKinsey Report, 21 million jobs will be needed by 2020 for the U.S. economy to return to full employment.[1] Brand new jobs are most likely to come from brand new industries, or brand new directions in existing industries. New employment opportunities can be sparked by investors seeing an opportunity to make money by building the capacity to sell lots of new things that consumers haven't yet realized they want. One potential innovation platform, believe it or not, is our car's fuel tank, and the new things are non-petroleum fuels. The iPhone equivalent in the transportation sector is the flexible fuel vehicle.

The flex fuel vehicle

To the untrained eye, a flex fuel vehicle (FFV) looks exactly like a regular gasoline-only car. What gives it away in some cases is a small plate in the rear and a bright yellow gas cap. That's about all. The rest - an optical sensor which determines the alcohol-gasoline ratio, an algorithm in the computer that controls the car's electronic fuel injector and adjusts the air/fuel ratio accordingly and a set of seals made from a type of plastic that is resistant to corrosive alcohol - happens pretty much under the hood. The flex fuel engine can burn any blend of gasoline, ethanol and methanol. No matter what ratio is used, the engine will know how to optimize its performance. A driver could start his journey with a tank full of gasoline and refuel on the way with different types of alcohol at any blend and without having to measure the ratio.

Today, our cars are the equivalent of individuals with severe food allergies. Let's say you were allergic to milk and every dairy product. In fact, the only kind of "milk" you could safely drink is made of made from soy, yet, you'd like to start every morning with a cup of coffee with some milk in it. Soy milk could go to $50 a gallon and you still could not purchase cow's milk or goat milk in its stead. All you could do is scrimp and save and make do with less soy milk in your coffee. Take a look at the figure below. This graph compares the per energy unit (i.e., the per-mile) price of gasoline as compared to methanol over the past five years for a variety of oil and natural gas prices. You'll notice that most of the time, on a per-mile basis methanol was less expensive than gasoline. But we couldn't make an on the fly choice to fuel with it, because cars that are not fuel flexible are in essence allergic to anything other than gasoline. It doesn't matter how expensive oil (and thus gasoline) gets, or how inexpensive natural gas (and thus methanol) becomes. With non-flexible cars, all we can do is scrimp and save and put less gasoline in our tanks. We can't just pour in another fuel instead.

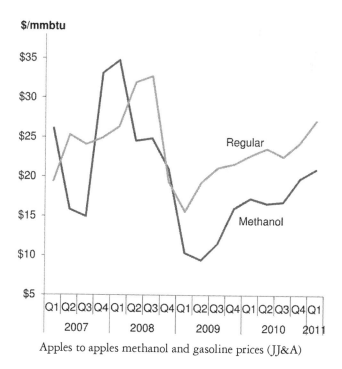

Apples to apples methanol and gasoline prices (JJ&A)

Fuel flexibility is a very inexpensive feature. According to General Motors' Vice Chairman Tom Stevens, flex-fuel systems currently add a premium of around $70 to the cost of a regular vehicle.[2] But for this cost GM warranties the car to run only on blends of gasoline and ethanol. While perhaps satisfying to some in the ethanol industry who prefer to be a big fish in a small non-petroleum fuels market rather than brawl over market share with lots of other players, that's not sufficient for an open and competitive market. In order to open cars to real competition, flex fuel vehicles must be warrantied to run on gasoline, ethanol and methanol (GEM flexibility). Adding methanol capability, which will allow us to arbitrage fuel made from natural gas, coal, trash and biomass against fuels make from oil, does not add more than a handful of dollars to the price of each vehicle. And since methanol is the most corrosive of alcohols, ensuring cars can uses it technically opens them to a broad possible array of other fuels. According to the Sloan Automotive Laboratory at MIT, the incremental cost for a GEM vehicle is $90. The breakdown: $20 for the fuel sensor, $50 for the fuel system materials, and $20 for the catalyst in the evaporative system. If the automaker wanted to make a bigger fuel tank and pump to make up for the lower energy density of methanol so the car would have the same range, the MIT report specifies an additional expense of $120.[3] However, the automaker could just as well choose to keep the same size tank, and let consumers decide if they are willing to take on the range penalty (since methanol is less energy dense than gasoline) and refuel more often in order to save money per mile.

Despite the low cost of the FFV in comparison with other automotive technologies like hybridization, electrification, hydrogen and CNG, the automakers have been fiercely opposed to any statutory initiative to make fuel flexibility a standard feature in every new automobile. In 2011, a bipartisan group of legislators in the House and the Senate introduced the Open Fuel Standard Act, a bill requiring automakers to open new cars to fuel competition. In other words, to ensure that most light-passenger vehicles sold in the United States are capable of running on something else in addition to or instead of gasoline. While the bill is technology neutral, the cheapest option for enabling fuel competition by far is the flexible fuel engine. Shortly after the bill's introduction, sixteen trade associations representing the automotive industry and its allies fired off a letter urging members of Congress to oppose the bill on the grounds that it would cost consumers collectively more than a billion dollars per year to buy such vehicles. In a good year, the auto industry sells some 16 million cars in the U.S. In a bad year, that number shrinks to about 10 million. So that collective cost of a billion dollars per year, assuming the auto lobbyists writing the letter had the worst case in mind, equates to a cost of about $100 per car ($1 billion divided by 10 million.) Among the signatories were the Alliance of Automobile Manufacturers, the American Automotive Policy Council, the American International Automobile Dealers Association, the Association of Global Automakers, the Engine Manufacturers Association, the Motor & Equipment Manufacturers Association, the National Association of Manufacturers, the National Automobile Dealers Association, the Trucks Manufacturers Association and the all-powerful U.S. Chamber of Commerce.

There are various reasons for the opposition of these organizations to the Open Fuel Standard, some having to do with a general (and in most other situations well-based) aversion to government telling industry what to do, others with reluctance to spend money on fuels that are not currently generally available at fuel stations, and some with a false perception that the bill is yet another giveaway to the hated ethanol industry. But it would be in the economic interest of the auto industry to support widespread fuel competition, as will be elaborated below.

Making fuel flexibility a standard feature in new cars is a prerequisite to broad availability of competing fuels at fuel stations. A fuel station that has say 10 pumps will not see a business case for retrofitting one (or installing a new one) to sell a competing fuel until and unless some 15-20 percent of the cars in its area can use that fuel. Retrofitting an existing 10,000 gallon gasoline pump and tank to serve methanol would cost $19,000-$30,000 including labor. To install a completely new system rather than retrofit an existing one would cost about $60,000. These are not huge sums but service station owners would need to see good enough potential demand for, in this case methanol, to incur the expense and hassle of retrofitting their equipment. Throwing tax credits or grants at the station for this purpose will not change the situation. A fuel pump that sells a competing fuel is a waste of retail space unless there are enough cars in the area that can use that fuel and thus enough costumers with an interest in purchasing it. If most new cars are fuel flexible, given vehicle turnover times in the United States, within some three years that critical 15-percent-of-the-fleet threshold will be hit. The lack of competing fuels at pumps in the interim won't inconvenience drivers of fuel flexible cars – they can just fuel with gasoline until pumps offering other fuels are available.

At the same time, the standardization of fuel flexibility in cars would send a signal to investors that there is a profit opportunity in expanding production capacity for fuels that can compete with gasoline for a broad range of oil prices. Over time, this increase in production capacity would lead to a situation where these fuels compete for market share with oil. This competition would serve to drag down the price of oil to the $45-$50 per barrel price band where its competitors are just profitable. Nothing could be better for the auto industry, since the difference between a bad year where 10 million new cars are sold in the United States and a good year where 16 million cars are sold is in large part a function of oil price.

Lotus 270 Tri-fuel. It's a flex fuel vehicle
Courtesy: Lotus Engineering

Cheap fuel is good for Detroit

Other than the airline industry, no industry suffers from high oil prices more than the auto industry. When oil prices rise the economy slows down and Americans have less disposable income with which to purchase new vehicles. The cars they do buy tend to be smaller and cheaper. Since Detroit makes most of its profits on light trucks and SUVs its profits take a hit when oil prices soar.[4] In the long run sustained high gasoline prices have a lasting effect on the automakers' bottom lines. When fuel prices are high, people drive fewer miles and that means less wear and tear, less replacement parts and fewer road accidents. All of those mean slower vehicle replacement and hence less profit for Detroit.

Expensive fuel is therefore a drag on the autos' financial well-being. By any yardstick the industry would be better off when fuel prices are low. As shown below the impact of oil price spikes on new vehicle sales is drastic. Following the 1973 oil embargo new vehicles sales in the United States dropped by 23 percent. The 1979 oil shock delivered a 32 percent decline; and the Great Recession collapsed auto sales by 37 percent. Since oil prices began their upward movement in 2004 and until the financial crash in 2008, Ford lost two thirds of its share value. GM and Chrysler fared even worse. In 2009, they both filed for Chapter 11, and their stocks were delisted from the New York Stock Exchange. In light of the strong causality between high oil prices and dips in automobile sales, it is hard to understand why the automakers wouldn't take every measure they can to help reduce the cost of fuel and even more so why they insist on fighting the only near term policy that can protect them against crippling oil shocks. To better understand the enigma one should revisit Detroit's opposition to an earlier federal mandate – on airbags.

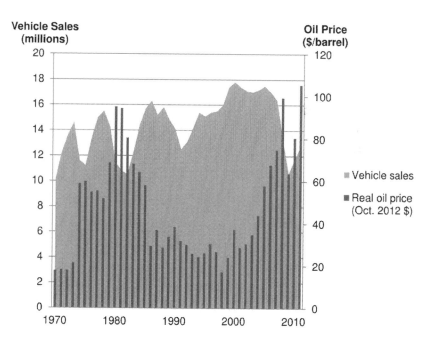

The impact of high oil prices on vehicle sales

Lessons from the airbag debate

Since the 1960s, car safety was a matter of national controversy. America became a nation of motorists, but with increased car ownership came rising social costs associated with countless injuries and fatalities from road accidents. In 1966, the number of fatalities on America's roads reached the ominous number of 50,000, five times the number of military deaths in Vietnam for that year. In 1968, the federal government mandated that all new cars must be equipped with seat belts. The automakers were strongly opposed. They disliked the added cost but even more so they felt safety wouldn't sell and that highlighting seatbelts would invoke drivers' fears about being trapped in burning cars or underwater. Hard to believe, but getting the automakers to install seatbelts was easy in comparison to getting people to buckle up. Seatbelt use in the United States ranged between 3 and 10 percent.[5] And bad habits, as we know, die hard. So in the early 1970s, GM and Ford started to experiment with airbags, a small box with sensors installed on the steering wheel that would automatically deploy an air cushion in case of collision and hence protect the vehicle's occupants. The autos may have had no intention of introducing them en masse throughout their product line, but the invention caught the attention of road safety advocates who demanded that airbags become a standard feature, just like seatbelts. A fierce public debate erupted. One side held that safety is a personal responsibility, and the individual has to take full precautions to ensure his or her own safety. Those on the other side of the debate held that since too many individuals do not behave responsibly, inflicting cost on their surroundings, there is a need for a technical fix that would ensure their maximum safety as well as the safety of those who might be casualties of their irresponsible behavior. Each side presented the government with studies and expert opinions to bolster their case. It was not only a debate about money but also about personal responsibility and the role of government in ensuring public safety, a debate between those who believed in technical fixes and those who believed in behavioral changes, such as encouraging the use of seatbelts. Naturally, the automakers played a pivotal role in the dispute. They were squarely against an airbag mandate not only because of the extra cost involved and the hassle of reengineering the steering wheel and front compartments of all of their vehicles but also due to their concern that the widespread use of airbags would open them up to a wide array of legal liabilities. Each accident with fatalities or injuries could potentially be grounds for lawsuit. For their part, the automakers insisted that safety should be squarely the responsibility of motorists who should strap themselves to their seat instead of relying on the airbag panacea. The automakers, who a decade earlier fought seatbelts tooth and nail, were now clinging to the technology as a guard against the bigger evil - the airbag. It didn't help. In 1970, the National Highway Safety Bureau issued a regulation which essentially mandated airbags. The automakers took the government to court, claiming that the technology the agency demanded was "not feasible."[6] Changes of administrations and court battles delayed the mandate, and the rest of the 1970s were years of stalemate. The tension began to dissipate in the mid-1980s when Mercedes introduced high end cars equipped with airbags to the U.S. market. What was different about Mercedes' approach was that their offering was not aimed to supplant seatbelts but to *supplement* them. Both technologies should be used simultaneously, the German automaker urged. In other words, Mercedes offered its customers an extra benefit - choice in safety. If you wanted to strap yourself in, the car offered you the option to do so, but if you chose not to do so, the airbag device was there, just in case. (Think plug-in hybrid: you can plug-in your car and enjoy driving on cheap electricity, but if you didn't you could still drive on liquid fuel; or think flex fuel vehicle: you can fuel it with another liquid if it's cheaper or you can stick to gasoline). What happened next was remarkable. One by one, automakers that previously were fiercely opposed to airbags began to install them voluntarily and even brag about the so called "Supplemental Restraint System." "Reframing the airbag as a supplement to – not a replacement of – the seatbelt made installing the technology a significantly more palatable idea for the automobile companies," wrote transportation technology expert Jameson Wetmore.[7] In essence what Mercedes did to break the stalemate was to redistribute responsibility, sharing it between drivers and the automakers. The automakers continued to stress the importance of buckling up but they offered safety conscious motorists an extra protective feature. Maintaining the emphasis on motorists' personal responsibility in using seatbelts reduced much of the liability concerns the automakers had. Simultaneously, in 1984 then Secretary of Transportation Elizabeth Dole introduced regulations that required all automakers offer protection that does not require any action by front seat vehicle occupants. The ruling stated that all cars from vehicle model year 1987 would be required to have either automatic seat belts or driver side air bags. The choice of which technology to use was left to the automakers. Most of them opted to use less expensive automatic seat belts rather than airbags during this time period. But the ruling came with a sweetener. Dole added a provision in which automakers would be exempted from the regulation if within five years two thirds of the nation would be covered by state seatbelt use mandates. This created a strong incentive for the autos to invest in public safety education and in lobbying state governments to pass seatbelt use laws. Both measures helped increase national seatbelt use from 14 percent in 1984 to 45 percent in 1989. Today the percentage of seatbelt users in the United States is 85 percent and growing.[8] We buckle up in our cars without putting much thought into it and tens of thousands of lives are saved annually. At the same time, all new vehicles sold in the United States are equipped with airbags further reducing crash fatalities. How did that come about? And what are the lessons for those of us today who would like to see choice in fuels?

The first lesson is shared responsibility. The automakers rejected a situation in which they were made to bear the entire responsibility, and potential legal liability, for passengers' safety. The automakers' opposition to airbags fizzled as consumers' interest in vehicle safety grew. As long as safety played a minor role in consumers' purchasing preference automakers could ignore it. Once consumers placed a higher value on safety, cars quickly became safer. Fuel competition faces a similar challenge. As long as consumers accept the single-fuel standard as a law of nature there will be no drive for change. Only when consumers view the ability to make an on the fly decision as to which fuel they would like to purchase as an imperative will they demand cars that allow it. Second, an atmosphere of distrust in which both sides hurl law suits against each other is not conducive to progress. Thousands of lives could have been saved in the 1970s through improved automobile safety had the discourse occurred in a more collaborative atmosphere. Only the introduction of out-of-the-box "third ways" by Mercedes and Secretary Dole created the conditions for progress. For the autos to accept the imperative of fuel competition and to be willing to make accommodations will require a vision of forward motion by other stakeholders: fuel producers expanding production of competing fuels, distributors easing the penetration of new fuels into their stations once enough cars are there to use them, and government agencies reducing red tape and speeding certification of various blends.

What the airbag case study teaches us is that the automakers' opposition to technology mandates is not necessarily derived from parsimony or a kneejerk reaction to government mandates but from wider calculations like risk aversion, exposure to litigation and a tendency to respond to consumers' demand rather than trying to shape it – that is, to follow the market rather than to lead it. To be sure, quarter to quarter thinking and general corporate inertia also play a role. There is generally no penalty for missing an opportunity in big corporate behemoths like auto companies, but there is a penalty for making a change and getting it wrong. When a defunct Chevy Volt battery burst in flames in a storage garage three weeks after a test collision, GM's leadership was summoned to a dress down in a Capitol Hill hearing (the brouhaha was really much ado about nothing; we assume in those three weeks all passengers had time to exit the vehicle, and in normal usage cases after an accident the battery would be dealt with appropriately). The EV-bashing media had a field day, and demand for the Volt slowed down so much that the company had to suspend its production temporarily. And that's without any loss of life or property. In such an environment, one can give the autos some slack for a lack of corporate gumption.

Between 2006 and 2008, the CEOs of the Big Three committed publicly – repeatedly – to make 50 percent of their new cars FFVs by 2012. "There is nothing that can be done which can reduce the curve of growth in imported oil and actually turn it down like using E85, taking advantage of what's there today," said Rick Wagoner, chief executive of GM.[9] (Methanol, Rick, methanol.) But this commitment came with a caveat: provided that enough fueling infrastructure develops.[10] When it comes to FFVs – a tweak by any yardstick – the industry's approach has been "show us the fuel and we will deliver the cars." This has been a convenient copout for the autos, one that enabled them to renege on their promise. The year 2012 came and went and less than 10 percent of the cars sold in the United States today are FFVs, and the share of FFVs of the total light duty vehicle fleet is under five percent. It is hard to see how fueling infrastructure could develop with such a low car density. In this chicken and egg-like car and fuel situation, it makes most sense for the cars to be the chicken. After all when someone decides to buy a new car for say, $12,000, the likelihood that raising the cost to $12,100 in order to allow fuel flexibility will change the purchase decision is vanishingly low (if it weren't, we would see more cars offered MAD magazine no-frills style without seat cushions, cup holders, and other such features.)

The CAFE credit

There is another reason automakers aren't enthusiastic about making fuel flexibility standard. As we can see in Table 8.1, more than half of the cars Americans purchased in 2010 were small and midsize cars. Yet, curiously only one tenth of GM's 30 FFV models catered to this market. In total, the Big Three offered fuel competition in these classes in only eight of the 50 FFV models they marketed. In other words, most of the FFV models that Detroit markets are large sedans, vans, pickup trucks and SUVs. In fact, two thirds of GM's FFV fleet have engines larger than five liters. The Chevrolet Silverado, the Ford F-150, the GMC Yukon, the Cadillac Escalade, even the Hummer H2 are all marketed as FFVs, albeit limited to gasoline and ethanol, and their owners can take advantage of a little bit of fuel choice. The same privilege is denied to the other half of vehicle purchasers who prefer smaller fuel efficient cars. The reason for this is embedded in the labyrinth of statutes and regulations that various Congresses and administrations have assembled over the years regarding requirements for fleet wide vehicle fuel efficiency.

Table 8.1: Detroit's FFV offering 2010

Class	Light vehicle market share[11]	Average engine size in liters	GM	Ford	Chrysler	Total Big Three
Small car	23.7%	2.41	-	-	-	-
Midsize car and wagon	27.3%	2.65	3	2	3	8
Large car	18.8%	3.34	5	3		8
Midsize van	3.4%	3.51	-	-	3	3
SUV	24.9%	3.98	11	4		15
Large van	0.1%	4.79	6	2	-	8
Pickup	12.6%	5.05	5	1	2	8
Total			30	12	8	50

In an attempt to encourage the widespread use of non-petroleum fuels and to promote the production of vehicles that can use them by auto manufacturers, Congress enacted the Alternative Motor Fuels Act (AMFA) in 1988. This law provides vehicle manufacturers with Corporate Average Fuel Economy (CAFE) credits for the production of vehicles capable of operating on non-petroleum fuels. When they add an FFV option the autos can collect credit (points, not dollars) that counts toward their overall CAFE requirement. This credit is limited in scope and at most can bump up the automakers average fleetwide fuel economy by 1.2 mpg. The results of the policy have been mixed. On the one hand this incentive program has been a major factor in driving the manufacture of the 50 or so models that can run today on non-petroleum fuels, mostly ethanol. But as we saw, what the program essentially did was to incentivize the autos to apply the FFV capability mostly to their heavier models like trucks and vans. If they didn't add the FFV capability, automakers would have to struggle more and spend more money to make cars more fuel efficient in order to meet their CAFE obligations. Whether or not the Hummer or the F-150 ends up using non-petroleum fuel is of no concern to the autos – indeed, until a recent federal law required it, most flex fuel vehicles were not even labeled as such so drivers had no idea they could put something else in their tank. The CAFE credit program has drawn fire from many fronts including environmentalists who see it as a way for the autos to get away with selling larger and larger gas guzzlers under the guise of a green product – "Live Green Go Yellow" was the slogan encouraging buyers to buy yellow capped E85 cars. A report to Congress by several government departments concluded that "unless the availability and use of alternative fuels is significantly expanded, the CAFE credit incentive program will not result in any reduced petroleum consumption or greenhouse gas emissions in the future."[12] Since the credit is limited in scope, automakers have for the most part made just enough cars fuel flexible to hit that 1.2 mpg credit limit, and thus the overall number of fuel flexible vehicles in the fleet is very small, far from enough for there to be a business case for fuel stations to sell an additional fuel.

With 54.5 mpg CAFE standards recently imposed on them, the automakers need the CAFE credit more than ever. They will not give it up easily. But as the details of the new CAFE rules are being hammered out, the incentive is likely to be diminished or discontinued altogether. The automakers' proclamations before Congress that they would equip 50 percent of their cars with flexible fuel engines are now being replaced with veiled threats that extension of the credit provision will be a major factor in their decision to continue offering vehicles that are fuel competitive. In this context, automakers are concerned that if fuel flexibility becomes a standard feature, Congress and/or the administration will see no reason to keep allowing them CAFE credits. Hence their opposition to an Open Fuel Standard. Congress and the administration will have to determine whether for achieving automaker buy-in for the standardization of fuel competition it is worth continuing the credit and perhaps even expanding it from 1.2 mpg to say three or five mpg should flexibility be expanded from GE (gasoline-ethanol) to GEM (gasoline-ethanol-methanol.) Considering the low likelihood of the automakers meeting their aggressive 54.5 mpg-by-2025 CAFE requirement, it may be a good deal for both consumers and the automakers themselves and, since the use of alcohol will result in greenhouse gas reduction, environmentalists would be smart to support this type of deal as well.

EPILOGUE
WHAT WOULD HAYEK DO?

The real problem we face over oil dates from after 1970: a strong but clumsy monopoly of mostly Middle Eastern exporters cooperating as OPEC. {...} Price fixing by private companies on the OPEC scale would not be tolerated in any industrial country. In the United States, the officers of firms that engage in such activities go to jail. But the OPEC members are sovereign states, subject to no country's laws.

MIT Professor of Economics Emeritus M.A. Adelman[1]

One of the greatest economists and political philosophers of the 20th century and the world's leading free market proponent was Nobel Laureate in Economics Friedrich August Hayek. Hayek grew up in Austria and as a 19-year old fought in World War I, an experience that shaped his thinking and drove him to examine how to prevent the repeat of such a calamity. After the war, he earned two doctorates and moved to New York. In 1929, he had his Nouriel Roubini moment when he warned about the imminent crash of the U.S. stock market several months before it actually happened. During the years of the Great Depression and the disputes over the New Deal, and even more so during the post-World War II years, Hayek became the chief intellectual opponent of the statist course set by Great Britain and others. He warned against the implications to freedom rooted in central planning as a supposed tool of combating the periodic market booms and busts. In this, Hayek was chief intellectual rival to John Maynard Keynes whose ideas called for overactive government and fiscal expansion. In 1945, Hayek published his triumphantly successful book *The Road to Serfdom,* a manifest in defense of markets and competition which made him the darling of conservative parties and leaders all over the world, including Margaret Thatcher.

Unlike in a Soviet style state-directed, planned economy, in a market economy sellers and buyers determine prices individually and interactively minute by minute simply by acting in their own interests. Due to historical, political and structural reasons market forces are at times blocked from operating the way they should. One common form of market failure Hayek warned against is the creation of monopolies and cartels. Hayek would have detested the OPEC oil cartel, which collectively acts as a monopolist in the oil market. As he wrote, "Our freedom of choice in a competitive society rests on the fact that, if one person refuses to satisfy our wishes, we can turn to another. But if we face a monopolist, we are at his mercy."[2]

What would Hayek have thought about "doing something" to counter OPEC? Like most prominent champions of free enterprise, he saw a role for government in strengthening market forces, among other things by dealing with monopolies. In a speech before the Economic Club of Detroit he stated, "We cannot seriously argue that government ought to do nothing."[3]

But what ought government to do? Some free market advocates believe that all that is required to make OPEC irrelevant is to lift all regulations on oil exploration and drilling in the United States. Would that were the case. Unfortunately, geology won't cooperate. As BP reports in its 2012 Statistical Review of World Energy, the United States has 1.9 percent of the world's proved oil reserves. Proved reserves mean "those quantities that geological and engineering information indicates with reasonable certainty can be recovered in the future from known reservoirs under existing economic and operating conditions" – in other words, basically conventional oil, tar sands, and tight oil.[4] Oil moves from the "resources" category to the "Proven Reserves" category once it becomes technically (not legally, but technically) possible to extract it at an economically realistic price point. Claims by some politicians and political activists that "we have more oil in this country than in Saudi Arabia"[5] are due to either wishful thinking and demagoguery, or innocent confusion between two very different resources with similar sounding names: tight oil from shale formations and shale oil. While the former is the type of liquid crude trapped within rock formations, which is now being extracted in North Dakota, the latter is crude extracted from hydrocarbon-rich rocks, and while there are some companies hard at work trying to develop ways to extract oil from those rocks, called oil shale, economically, those efforts are very much in their early stage, not sufficiently near an economic price point for extraction to be considered realistic. While we support reducing restrictions on drilling (not to mention other industrial activity) simply doing that will not be enough to counteract OPEC. At this point, we don't have the reserves that would enable a ramp up to sufficient production capacity to nullify OPEC's influence.

If OPEC were comprised of regular companies, the answer to what government ought to do would be obvious. This is what anti-trust actions are designed for. However, OPEC is comprised of sovereign regimes immune to such proceedings. So this leaves two options. The first, which we don't believe Hayek would have supported (and in any case would be a woefully unrealistic folly) would be to commit even more American and allied blood and treasure than has thus far been committed in the Persian Gulf and attempt to forcibly gain control of the oil reserves there. Perhaps this is what those individuals who sport "what is our oil doing under their soil" bumper stickers want (or perhaps they mean the opposite and we're misinterpreting their sarcasm.) Regardless of the dubious morality of such an action, its inefficacy should not be in doubt for a moment. We may indeed succeed in taking over the territory, but we will never succeed in getting access to the oil. It is simply too easy for insurgents to attack oil infrastructure. We tracked terrorist attacks against Iraqi oil pipelines, installations, and key industry personnel between January 2003 and the beginning of 2008 (we gave up at that point.) There were more than 450 attacks. That's about one every five days, and Iraq's oil production took a very long time to recover as a result.

This leaves one option. OPEC's monopolistic hold over the oil market would be made irrelevant if oil was just one of many commodities competing over the transportation fuel market. However, it is practically the only one. (As noted earlier, only one percent of U.S. electricity is generated from oil and only one percent of U.S. oil demand is due to electricity generation. Globally the numbers are similar. The oil story is about transportation.) Some free market advocates mistakenly believe that the lack of optionality in the transportation fuel market is due to the lack of economic appeal of other fuels. This is incorrect. Take another look at the graph in Chapter 8 showing the per energy unit (i.e., the per-mile) price of gasoline as compared to methanol over the past five years for a variety of oil and natural gas prices, and again notice that most of the time on a per-mile basis methanol was less expensive than gasoline. The single-fuel combustion engine prevents other fuels from competing with oil. The technical advantage given to petroleum based fuels by the automakers in essence forestalls entry of other fuels even when they are much less expensive. Today, when GM and Ford sell us a car that can run only on petroleum product they essentially mandate us to use one specific fuel – gasoline – no matter how competitive its competitors are. In other words, they are forcing us to buy an expensive fuel instead of a cheaper one. Thus, because of the single fuel engine, OPEC's position as a monopolist in the oil market also gives it the position of a monopolist in the transportation fuel market. Ubiquitous vehicle side fuel optionality would drive significant increases in production capacity for non-petroleum fuels because of the favorable economics of fuels like methanol. Eventually, production capacity for non-petroleum fuels would increase sufficiently that oil based fuels would face competition over fuel market share. Since competition among substitutable products is waged over price, this would serve to drag down the price of oil to the point where competing fuels are economic, namely a $45-$50 per barrel price band. As pointed out before, enabling liquid fuel competition would cost automakers on the order of $100 per new car. But is there a justification for forcing industry to open new cars to fuel competition? Why not leave it to the market to fix itself? If consumers demand a certain product why wouldn't the automakers respond to the need on their own volition?

What would Hayek have thought about an Open Fuel Standard requiring new cars to be open to fuel competition? His writing gives us a hint. Today, herd-like non-thinking conformism to rigid rules (eg. government should not require anything under any circumstances) without understanding the basic principles that underlie them, and thus the occasions in which circumstances demand a different response, has unfortunately become a feature of many politicians, pundits and hacks. In *The Road to Serfdom,* Hayek argued strongly against such four-legs-good-two-legs-bad thinking. In his words (note that Hayek's use of the term "liberal" refers to classical liberalism, the political ideology that advocates limited government, individual liberty and free enterprise):

> Probably nothing has done so much harm to the liberal cause as the wooden insistence of some liberals on certain rules of thumb, above all the principle of laissez-faire.[…] Against the innumerable interests which could show that particular measures would confer immediate and obvious benefits on some, while the harm they caused was much more indirect and difficult to see, nothing short of some hard-and-fast rule would have been effective. And since a strong presumption in favor of industrial liberty had undoubtedly been established, the temptation to present it as a rule which knew no exceptions was too strong always to be resisted.[6]

Those politicians that, in Hayek's words, woodenly insist on particular rigid rules of thumb regardless of the circumstances are in fact violating the very marrow of the ideology they think they uphold. Hayek accorded a certain, circumscribed role for government in the market, including as a counterweight to monopolistic coercion. Cars that block competing fuels are a barrier to the development of a free market in fuels. Other, less costly, fuels face a chicken and egg conundrum: why would fuel stations install pumps to serve them before cars are capable of handling them, and why would automakers enable their handling until they are available at stations? Something has got to give, and because of the low cost of enabling vehicle side fuel optionality, and the fact that drivers can still fuel with gasoline while the fueling infrastructure catches up, it makes sense to declare cars as the chicken. Given the absence of other options to break OPEC, and the strong national and economic interest in doing so, we believe Hayek would have supported the Open Fuel Standard.

He would not be alone in doing so. Hayek was a contemporary of another famous Austrian economist, Ludwig von Mises, who, too, alerted against the deep rooted forces hampering competition and free markets. "The forces aiming at a restriction of competition play a great role in our day. It is an important task of the history of our age to deal with them," he wrote.[7] Another luminary, Noble Laureate in Economics Milton Friedman, also preached for government action in the name of monopoly busting. Friedman believed that the most important and the strongest monopolies are those derived from government privileges and therefore because it is the government that created them it is the responsibility of government to kill them. He wrote that:

> [...] the role of government just considered is to do something that the market cannot do itself, namely, to determine, arbitrate, and enforce the rules of the game. We may also want to do through government some things that might conceivably be done through the market but that technical or similar conditions render it difficult to do in that way. These all reduce to cases in which strictly voluntary exchange is either exceedingly costly or practically impossible.[8]

A monopoly is exactly one such case. Friedman therefore concluded that "the first and most urgent necessity in the area of government policy is the elimination of those measures which directly support monopoly."[9] We cannot think of a product which supports monopoly, in this case OPEC's monopoly over the transportation fuel market, more than the petroleum-only vehicle.

Friedman, von Mises and Hayek acknowledged the dangers of an unattended imperfect market and the risks of unchallenged monopolists. But what was understood by 20th century free market theorists is not necessarily clear to present day politicians, some of whom are more anti-regulation than they are pro-market. There are good reasons for this. We live in an era in which many Americans are frustrated and resentful of the government's intervention in the economy. The government's record in picking technological winners from President Carter's Synthetic Fuels Corporation through President George W. Bush's "hydrogen economy" all the way to President Obama's Solyndra scandal leaves little taste for new taxpayer funded boondoggles. Billions of dollars have gone down the drain because members of Congress made flawed assumptions about the viability of one technology or another, about how the market might or might not work, or just because they simply failed to ask the right questions. But while the aversion to government intervention in the market is understood, it should not be turned into a religion. The intellectual inflexibility displayed in defense of the sacred principle of no-mandates is leading the United States to economic suicide. There is no gentler way of saying it: members of Congress – many of whom voted for mandates from digital television to rear end cameras in cars – who oppose measures that open the fuel market to competition are aiding and abetting OPEC and others who benefit from the single-fuel system. In the end, it is they who stand between the perpetuation of a restrictive, monopolistic and economically ruinous fuel system and a free and competitive fuel market which could provide us true and lasting energy security.

ABOUT THE AUTHORS

Anne Korin and Gal Luft are co-directors of the Institute for the Analysis of Global Security (IAGS), a Washington based think tank focused on energy security. They are also advisers to the United States Energy Security Council, America's highest level extra-governmental group focused on reducing the strategic importance of oil. They appear in the media frequently, testify before committees of the U.S. Congress and have written numerous articles for leading publications such as *Foreign Affairs, Foreign Policy, The American Interest, Commentary Magazine, The National Review, The Wall Street Journal,* and the *Washington Post*.

Their previous books are *Energy Security Challenges for the 21st Century* (2009) and *Turning Oil into Salt: Energy Independence through Fuel Choice* (2009).

You can visit IAGS at www.iags.org

NOTE ON THE COVER

The illustration on the cover was inspired by the late Yeshayahu Leibowitz' commentary on Genesis 11:1-9, the Tower of Babel episode. Leibowitz writes: "It appears to me that the root of the error, or sin, [...] was not the building of a city and tower, but the aim to use these artificial means to ensure a situation of "one language and one speech"- of centralization, which, in modern parlance, would be known as totalitarianism. One language and one speech is, according to many naive people in our days, a description of an ideal situation: all of humanity a single bloc, without differentiation, and, as a result, without conflicts. But one who truly understands will know that there is nothing which is more threatening than this artificial conformism: a city and tower as the symbol of the concentration of all of mankind about a single topic- where there will not be differences of opinion and there will not be a struggle over different viewpoints and over different values. One cannot imagine greater tyranny than that, one cannot imagine a greater mental and moral sterility than that-that there should be no exceptions and that there should be no deviations from what is accepted and agreed upon, and this being maintained by the artificial means of a city and a tower. In His mercy and compassion for mankind, God prevented this from occurring, and He made a humanity where a totalitarianism of complete unity cannot be."

Source: Yeshayahu Leibowitz, *Accepting the Yoke of Heaven,* (Urim Publications 2002)

ENDNOTES

Prologue

[1] President Ronald Reagan, Farewell Address to the Nation, Oval Office, January 11, 1989

Introduction

Barking Up the Wrong Tree

[1] Gal Luft and Anne Korin, *Turning Oil into Salt: Energy Independence through Fuel Choice*, (Booksurge, 2009.)

[2] Charles J. Cicchetti and Willian J. Gillen, "The Mandatory Oil Import Quota Program: A Consideration of Economic Efficiency and Equity," *Natural Resources Journal*, July 1973.

[3] President Richard Nixon's State of the Union Address, January 30, 1974, http://www.presidency.ucsb.edu/ws/index.php?pid=4327

[4] President Gerald Ford's State of the Union Address, January 15, 1975, http://www.ford.utexas.edu/library/speeches/750028.htm

[5] President Gerald Ford's State of the Union Address, January 19, 1976, http://www.ford.utexas.edu/library/speeches/760019.htm

[6] Speech by President Jimmy Carter, July 15, 1979, http://www.pbs.org/wgbh/americanexperience/features/primary-resources/carter-crisis/

[7] Remarks and a Question-and-Answer Session on the Program for Economic Recovery at a Breakfast for Newspaper and Television News Editors, February 19, 1981

[8] President George Herbert Walker Bush, First State of the Union Address, February 9, 1989, http://www.presidency.ucsb.edu/ws/index.php?pid=16660

[9] President Bill Clinton, Statement on Energy Security, February 16, 1995

[10] "President Bush's State of the Union Address," *Washington Post*, January 31, 2006

[11] Remarks by President Barack Obama on Jobs, Energy Independence, and Climate Change, January 26, 2009

[12] Michael Mandelbaum, "Why the U.S. Must Make the Middle East Less Important," *Time Magazine*, August 12, 2010, http://www.time.com/time/magazine/article/0,9171,2010215,00.html

[13] Energy Information Administration, http://www.eia.gov/totalenergy/data/monthly/pdf/sec3_7.pdf

[14] "U.S. new car gas mileage up 20 percent since 2007: study," *Reuters,* April 1, 2012, http://www.reuters.com/article/2012/04/10/us-autos-fuel-idUSBRE8390UH20120410

[15] Energy Information Administration, *2011 Annual Energy Outlook,* Table 11, http://www.eia.gov/forecasts/aeo/tables_ref.cfm, International Energy Agency, *World Energy Outlook 2010,* p. 134, OPEC, *World Oil Outlook,* Chapter 8, http://www.opec.org/opec_web/en/publications/340.htm, and BP, *Energy Outlook 2030,* p. 72, www.bp.com/energyoutlook2030

[16] Leonardo Maugeri, "Global Oil Production is Surging: Implications for Prices, Geopolitics, and the Environment," Policy Brief, Belfer Center for Science and International Affairs, Harvard Kennedy School, June 2012, http://belfercenter.ksg.harvard.edu/files/maugeri_policybrief.pdf

[17] "US Inches toward Energy Independence," *New York Times,* March 22, 2012, http://www.nytimes.com/2012/03/23/business/energy-environment/inching-toward-energy-independence-in-america.html?_r=1

[18] Gal Luft and Anne Korin, *Turning Oil into Salt: Energy Independence through Fuel Choice,* (Booksurge, 2009)

[19] Alberto Salvo and Cristian Huse, "Is Arbitrage Tying the Price of Ethanol to that of Gasoline? Evidence from the Uptake of Flexible-Fuel Technology," October 2010, http://www.kellogg.northwestern.edu/faculty/salvo/htm/arbitrage.pdf

[20] Ibid.

[21] Congressional Budget Office, *Effects of Gasoline Prices on Driving Behavior and Vehicle Markets,* January 2008, http://www.cbo.gov/ftpdocs/88xx/doc8893/Summary.4.1.shtml

[22] "Iran Ends Gasoline Subsidies – But to what Effect?," Center for Global Energy Studies, July 2011, http://www.cges.co.uk/resources/articles/2011/07/12/iran-end-gasoline-subsidies-%E2%80%93-but-to-what-effect

[23] "Price tag of 2025's fuel efficiency standards: $157 billion," *Detroit News,* November 16, 2011, http://detnews.com/article/20111116/AUTO01/111160442/Price-tag-of-2025%E2%80%99s-fuel-efficiency-standards–$157-billion

[24] Ecuador actually rejoined OPEC in 2007; it had left the organization in 1992

[25] Newt Gingrich, *Drill Here, Drill Now, Pay Less: A Handbook for Slashing Gas Prices and Solving our Energy Crisis,* (Washington, DC: Regnery 2008), p.6

[26] Mandelbaum, "Why the U.S. Must Make the Middle East Less Important."

[27] Thomas Friedman, "Win, Win, Win, Win, Win...," *New York Times,* December 27, 2008, http://www.nytimes.com/2008/12/28/opinion/28friedman.html

28   Charles Krauthammer, "A net Zero Gas Tax, A-Once-in-a-Generation Chance," *The Weekly Standard*, January 5, 2009, http://www.weeklystandard. com/Content/Public/Articles/000/000/015/949rsrgi.asp

Chapter 1

Cartel and Barrel: Why OPEC *Does* Matter?

1   The Oil Kingdom, *CBS News*, *60 Minutes*, December 8, 2008, http://www. cbsnews.com/video/watch/?id=4653109n

2   Nael Shehadah, "Economic Costs, the Arab Spring and the GCC," Gulf Research Center Foundation, November 24, 2011

3   "Private Sector in Iraq: Creating Jobs and Enhancing Sustainable Development?", *Iraq Insights*, July 2011, http://www.ideas-synergy.net/wp-content/uploads/2011/09/Iraq-Insights-by-Ideas-sYnergy_July-2011 Issue-2.pdf

4   "Saudi needs oil above $49 to avoid deficit; Qatar break-even $24: IMF," *Gulf Times*, September 21, 2008, http://www.gulf-times.com/site/topics/article. asp?cu_no=2&item_no=242775&version=1&template_id=48&parent_ id=28

5   "OPEC Nations Face a Balancing Act," *Wall Street Journal*, April 19, 2011, http://online.wsj.com/article/SB100014240527487040040045762702515102 21730.html

6   Population Reference Bureau, 2009 World Population Data sheet, http:// www.prb.org/pdf09/09wpds_eng.pdf

7   Yadullah Ijtehadi, "Saudi Arabia's Other Major Crisis," Economic Monitor, July 27, 2011, http://www.economonitor.com/blog/2011/07/saudi-arabia%E2%80%99s-other-major-crisis/

8   Jim Krane, "The End of Saudi Oil Reserve Margin," *Wall Street Journal*, April 3, 2012, http://online.wsj.com/article/SB10001424052702303816504577319571732227492.html?mod=googlenews_wsj

9   "Report: Saudi oil exports declining due to domestic demand," *Oil and Gas Journal*, July 21, 2011.

10   "WikiLeaks cables: Saudi Arabia cannot pump enough oil to keep a lid on prices," *The Guardian*, February 8, 2011, http://www.guardian.co.uk/business/2011/feb/08/saudi-oil-reserves-overstated-wikileaks?intcmp=239

11   See Gal Luft and Anne Korin, "The Sino Saudi Connection," *Commentary Magazine* 2004 and "Islam's Divide and Us," *Commentary Magazine*, August 2007

12   "Saudi prince calls for lower oil prices," *CNN*, May 29, 2011, http://articles. cnn.com/2011-05-29/world/us.saudi.prince.oil_1_oil-prices-saudi-arabia-saudi-people?_s=PM:WORLD

13 "Russia May Face Debt Crisis Like Greece," *Bloomberg*, June 23, 2011, http://www.bloomberg.com/news/2011-06-23/russia-may-face-debt-crisis-like-greece-by-2030-world-bank-says.html

14 "OPEC is Irrelevant," *Newsweek*, July 31, 2008

15 "The FP Survey: Energy," *Foreign Policy*, July/August 2012, http://www.foreignpolicy.com/articles/2012/06/18/the_fp_survey_on_energy?page=0,5

16 Yoweri Museveni, "The Qaddafi I Know," *Foreign Policy*, March 24, 2011, http://www.foreignpolicy.com/articles/2011/03/24/the_qaddafi_I_know

17 Janine P. Roberts, *Glitter and Greed: The Secret World of the Diamond Cartel*, (NY: The Disinformation Company 2003,) p. 86

18 Leo, Drollas, "OPEC's Failure to Act Contributes to Worsening Global Economy," *Global Oil Insight*, August 2011

19 "$100/b oil good for consumers, producers: Al-Assaf," *Saudi Gazette*, April 28, 2012

20 "Saudi Oil Minister Discusses Rise in Prices," Saudi Embassy Press Release, March 8, 2011, http://saudiembassy.net/press-releases/press03081101.aspx

21 "Saudis Warned U.S. about Oil Speculators, Cables Show," *HeraldNet.com*, May 25, 2011, http://www.heraldnet.com/article/20110525/NEWS02/110529922

22 "Saudis Put Oil Capacity Rise on Hold," *Financial Times*, April 21, 2008

Chapter 2

The Making and Breaking of Petropoly

1 Randal O'Toole, *Gridlock: Why We're Stuck in Traffic and What to Do About It*, (Washington, DC: Cato Institute, 2010,) p.7-9

2 Joel Tarr and Clay McShane, "The Centrality of the Horse to the Nineteenth-Century American City," in Raymond Mohl, ed., *The Making of Urban America*, (NY: SR Publishers 1997), pp. 105-130

3 Edwin Black, *Internal Combustion: How Corporations and Governments Addicted the World to Oil and Derailed the Alternatives*, (NY: St. Martin's Press, 2006), p. 40

4 Tarr and McShane, pp. 105-130

5 "Automobile," *Encyclopedia Britannica*, http://www.britannica.com/EBchecked/topic/44957/automobile/259061/Early-electric-automobiles#ref=ref918099

6 Bill Kovarick, *Henry Ford, Charles Kettering and the "Fuel of the Future,"* 1998, http://www.radford.edu/wkovarik/papers/fuel.html#tax

7 "President Flays the Oil Trust," *Washington Post*, May 5, 1906

8 Edwin Black, *Internal Combustion*, p. 1

[9] Ibid

[10] American Petroleum Institute 1933 memo cited in Bill Kovarick, *Henry Ford, Charles Kettering and the "Fuel of the Future."* The original reference can be found in Harry Benge Crozier, Director of Public Relations to members of the public relations advisory committee, American Petroleum Institute, April 24, 1933, Series 4 Box 52, J. Howard Pew papers, Hagley Museum and Library, Wilmington, Del.

[11] Daniel Yergin, *The Prize*, p.230

[12] Olin T. Mouzon, "Petroleum Import Policy of the United States," *Economic Geography*, Vol. 22, No. 2 (Apr., 1946), pp. 116-125.

[13] U.S.-China Economic and Security Review Commission, Report to Congress 2002, http://www.uscc.gov/annual_report/2002/anrp02.php

[14] Totally Different, *Economist*, January 12, 2008

[15] Robert C. McFarlane and R. James Woolsey, "How to Weaken the Power of Foreign Oil," *New York Times*, September 20, 2011, http://www.usesc.org/energy_security/NYTSept212011.pdf

Chapter 3

America's Natural Gas: Hope and Change

[1] Rex W. Tillerson, Chairman and CEO, Exxon Mobil Corporation, Speech before the Council on Foreign Relations, June 27, 2012, http://www.cfr.org/united-states/new-north-american-energy-paradigm-reshaping-future/p28630

[2] "Greenspan Warns of 'Serious' Natgas Problems," *Reuters,* May 23, 2003.

[3] "Chemical Industry in Crisis," Washington Post, March 16, 2004, http://www.washingtonpost.com/wp-dyn/articles/A64579-2004March16_2.html

[4] John Hofmeister interview, Washington DC, September 21, 2011.

[5] Senator James Inhofe, "Energy and the Environment: The Future of Natural Gas," Senate Committee of Environment and Public Work, June 2005, http://epw.senate.gov/repwhitepapers/Energy.pdf

[6] "USGS boosts amount of Marcellus Shale gas reserves," *Wall Street Journal,* August 23, 2011, http://online.wsj.com/article/AP2d29300efb9c4a59a4a36048b28374d2.html

[7] U.S. Energy Information Administration, *Annual Energy Outlook 2012* and "Technically Recoverable Shale Gas Resources Jump 134 Percent," Institute for Energy Research, May 16, 2011, http://www.instituteforenergyresearch.org/2011/05/16/technically-recoverable-shale-gas-resources-jump-134-percent/

8   *Are We Entering a Golden Age of Gas?* International Energy Agency, Special Report, 2011 http://www.iea.org/weo/docs/weo2011/WEO2011_GoldenAgeofGasReport.pdf

9   David Brooks, "The Shale Gas Revolution," *New York Times*, November 3, 2011, http://www.nytimes.com/2011/11/04/opinion/brooks-the-shale-gas-revolution.html

10 Fareed Zakaria, "Natural Gas, Fueling an Economic Revolution," *Washington Post*, March 29, 2012, http://www.washingtonpost.com/opinions/shale-gas-an-alternative-to-oil-that-is-bolstering-the-us-economy/2012/03/29/gIQA-kIc7iS_story.html

11 "Unconventional Natural Gas: The U.S. Experience and Global Energy Security," Remarks by Robert Cekuta, Deputy Assistant Secretary, Bureau of Economic, Energy and Business Affairs, Address to the 2nd U.S.-Indonesia Energy Investment Roundtable, Jakarta, Indonesia, February 6, 2012, http://www.state.gov/e/enr/rls/rem/2012/183875.htm

12 Ian Ubrina, "Insiders Sound an Alarm Amid a Natural Gas Rush," *New York Times*, June 25, 2011, http://www.nytimes.com/2011/06/26/us/26gas.html?pagewanted=all

13 "Clinton Seeks Energy Fund Financed by Oil companies," *Bloomberg*, May 23, 2006, http://www.bloomberg.com/apps/news?pid=newsarchive&sid=a2dyHBGYynbM&refer=top_world_news

14 "Shell: We'll produce more gas than oil by 2012," CNN Money, http://money.cnn.com/2010/12/15/news/companies/shell-oil-gas-odum.fortune/index.htm

15 "Chesapeake Tackles Oversupply Issue," *Financial Times*, January 24, 2012, http://www.ft.com/intl/cms/s/0/6f8c32fe-46a4-11e1-89a8-00144feabdc0.html

16 "Shale-Gas Drilling to Add 870,000 U.S. Jobs by 2015, Report Says," *Bloomberg,* December 12, 2011, http://www.businessweek.com/news/2011-12-12/shale-gas-drilling-to-add-870-000-u-s-jobs-by-2015-report-says.html

17 "Refining Puts Lid on Big Oil's Profits," Wall Street Journal, January 23, 2012, http://online.wsj.com/article/SB100014240529702037504045771711 82994597996.html

18 Oil shale and shale oil are not the same, though they have been much confused by some politicians and pundits. See Note on Terminology for a fuller explanation.

19 *Future of Natural Gas*, MIT, http://web.mit.edu/mitei/research/studies/documents/natural-gas-2011/NaturalGas_Chapter5_Demand.pdf

Chapter 4

The Time Factor

[1] Tad Briend, "Plugged In," *The New Yorker*, August 24, 2009, http://www. newyorker.com/reporting/2009/08/24/090824fa_fact_friend

[2] Thomas Friedman, "Their Moon Shot and Ours," *New York Times*, September 25, 2010, http://www.nytimes.com/2010/09/26/opinion/26friedman.html?_ r=2&src=tptw

[3] Satoru Oyama, *Strong Growth to Drive Lithium-ion Battery Market to $54 Billion by 2020*, Rechargeable battery special report - 2011, IHS Report.

[4] "Top 5 Investment Trends of 2011," *Financial Edge*, January 25, 2011, http:// financialedge.investopedia.com/financial-edge/0111/Top-5-Investment-Trends-For-2011.aspx

[5] *Impacts Assessment of Plug-in Hybrid Vehicles on Electric Utilities and Regional Power Grids*, Pacific Northwest National Laboratory, November, 2007.

[6] S. W. Hadley and A. Tsvetkova, *Potential Impacts of Plug-in Hybrid Electric Vehicles on Regional Power Generation*, (Oak Ridge, TN: Oak Ridge National Laboratory, 2008)

[7] The President first announced this goal as a candidate in a speech in Lansing, Michigan on August 4, 2008. http://my.barackobama.com/page/ community/post/stateupdates/gG5zCW. He first reiterated the goal as president at a speech in Pomona, California on March 19, 2009. http://www. energy.gov/7067.htm.

[8] John Sausanis, "World Vehicle Population Tops 1 Billion Units," *Wardsauto. com*, August 15, 2011, http://wardsauto.com/ar/world_vehicle_population_110815/

[9] "Production plans for electric vehicles announced to date are below sales targets set by countries," International Energy Agency, July 5, 2011 http:// www.iea.org/index_info.asp?id=2044

[10] The National Academies, *Transition to Alternative Transportation Technologies – Plug-in Hybrid Electric Vehicles*, 2010; Deloitte, *Gaining traction: A customer view of electric vehicle mass adoption in the U.S. automotive market*, 2010, http://www.deloitte.com/assets/Dcom-UnitedStates/Local%20Assets/ Documents/us_automotive_Gaining%20Traction%20FINAL_061710. pdf; Energy Information Administration, *Annual Energy Outlook 2011 with Projections to 2035*, DOE/EIA-0383(2011), April 2011; Boston Consulting Group, *The Comeback of the Electric Car? How Real, How Soon and What Must Happen Next*, 2010, http://www.bcg.com/documents/file15404.pdf ; Credit Suisse, *Electric Vehicles: Back to the Future*, 2009, http://www.miaccess24.com/ chargeaccess24/electricvehicles.pdf ; IHS Global Insight, Battery Electric

and Plug-in Hybrid Vehicles: The Definitive Assessment of the Business Case, 2010.

11 "Over Time, Allure of Hybrid Ownership Wanes," *New York Times*, April 11, 2012, http://wheels.blogs.nytimes.com/2012/04/11/polk-study-over-time-allure-of-hybrid-ownership-wanes/

12 J.D. Power and Associates Reports: Future Global Market Demand for Hybrid and Battery Electric Vehicles May Be Over-Hyped; Wild Card is China, October 27, 2010, http://businesscenter.jdpower.com/news/pressrelease.aspx?ID=2010213

13 U.S. Energy Information Administration, Annual Energy Outlook 2011 (Washington, DC: U.S. Department of Energy, 2011).

14 "Is the moment for electric cars finally driving up?" *McClatchy Newspapers*, April 4, 2011, http://www.mcclatchydc.com/2011/04/04/111483/is-the-moment-for-electric-cars.html

15 Jim Motavalli, "China to Subsidize Electric Cars and Hybrids," *New York Times*, June 2, 2010, http://wheels.blogs.nytimes.com/2010/06/02/china-to-start-pilot-program-providing-subsidies-for-electric-cars-and-hybrids/

16 Chuck Squatriglia, "Shai Agassi Wants to Sell Electric Cars Like Cell Phones," *Wired Magazine*, October 30, 2007, http://www.wired.com/autopia/2007/10/selling-electri/

17 Ibid

18 Thomas Friedman, "Their Moon Shot and Ours," *New York Times*, September 25, 2010, http://www.nytimes.com/2010/09/26/opinion/26friedman.html?_r=2&src=tptw

19 Interview with Wolfgang Bernhart from Roland Berger Strategy Consultants, EV Update, June 12, 2012, http://analysis.evupdate.com/batteries-power-trains/wolfgang-bernhart-battery-costs

20 "E-Mobility and the Li-Ion Batteries – A Glimpse in the Future," Roland Berger Strategy Consultants, Presentation at the Technology and Rare Earth Metals Conference, Washington DC, March 13, 2012.

21 Katie Fehrenbacher, "Want Moore's Law for Batteries? Go Find An Asteroid," Gigaom.com, October 6, 2010.

22 Powertrain 2020: The Li-Ion Battery Value Chain, Trends and Implications, Roland Berger Strategy Consultants, August 2011, http://www.rolandberger.com/media/pdf/Roland_Berger_The_Li_Ion_Battery_Value_Chain_20110801.pdf

23 "Battery Technology Charges Ahead," *McKinsey Quarterly*, July 2012, https://www.mckinseyquarterly.com/Battery_technology_charges_ahead_2997 and "Electric vehicle battery prices down 14% year on year," Bloomberg New Energy Finance press release, April 16, 2012 http://www.bnef.com/PressReleases/view/210

24 "How Green Are Electric Cars? Depend on Where you Plug in," *New York Times*, April 13, 2012, http://www.nytimes.com/2012/04/15/automobiles/how-green-are-electric-cars-depends-on-where-you-plug-in.html?pagewanted=all

25 "The Electric Car, Unplugged," *New York Times*, March 24, 2012, http://www.nytimes.com/2012/03/25/sunday-review/the-electric-car-unplugged.html?_r=1

26 If you haven't read Orwell's *Animal Farm*, there's no time like the present.

27 Newt Gingrich: "You Can't Put a Gun Rack in a Volt," *USA Today*, February 21, 2012, http://content.usatoday.com/communities/driveon/post/2012/02/newt-gingrich-chevrolet-volt-gun-rack-romney-santorum/1

28 Edwin Black, Internal Combustion, p. 104

Chapter 5

The Rearden Metal of Fuels

1 "Fact sheet: Converting light duty vehicles to natural gas," Natural Gas Vehicles For America, http://www.ngvc.org/pdfs/FAQs_Converting_to_NGVs.pdf

2 Sonia Yeh, "Empirical Analysis on the Adoption of Alternative Fuel Vehicles: The Case for Natural Gas Vehicles," *Energy Policy* 35 (11) 5865-5875, 2007

3 Natural Gas Vehicles Journal, http://www.ngvjournal.dreamhosters.com/en/statistics/item/911-worldwide-ngv-statistics (Retrieved April 8, 2012)

4 National Petroleum Council, Vehicle and Fuel System Analyses, Natural Gas Analysis, August 1, 2012, p. NG61, http://www.npc.org/FTF-report-080112/Natural_Gas_Analysis-080112.pdf

5 U.S. Department of Energy, Alternative Fuels Data Center Website, www.eere.energy.gov/afdc/fuels/stations_counts.html, April 2012.

6 National Petroleum Council, Vehicle and Fuel System Analyses, Natural Gas Analysis, August 1, 2012, p. NG22, http://www.npc.org/FTF-report-080112/Natural_Gas_Analysis-080112.pdf, see also G.A. Wyatt, "Issues Affecting the Adoption of Natural Gas Fuel in Light- and Heavy-Duty Vehicles," U.S. Department of Energy report no. PNNL-19745 (September 2010).

7 Energy Information Administration, *Annual Energy Outlook 2010 with Projections to 2035*, p. 34 and Energy Information Administration, *Annual Energy Outlook 2011 with Projections to 2035*.

8 "Pickens' Plan No Longer Features Wind Energy," *NBC 10*, December 14, 2010, http://www.nbcphiladelphia.com/news/business/Pickens_Plan_no_longer_features_wind_energy-111852919.html

9   "Boone Doggle," *Wall Street Journal*, February 28, 2012.

10 Thomas Pyle, "NATGAS ACT: Déjà vu all over again," *The Hill*, September 21, 2011, http://thehill.com/blogs/congress-blog/energy-a-environment/183055-nat-gas-act-deja-vu-all-over-again

11 U.S. Energy Information Administration, based on U.S. Department of Energy (DOE), Alternative Fuels & Advanced Vehicles Data Center, as of March 27, 2012, http://www.afdc.energy.gov/afdc/

12 *American, Abundant... and Affordable?: A Cost Analysis of Natural Gas Vehicles (NGVS) and Fueling Infrastructure*, Autogas for America, http://autogasforamerica.org/pdf/Alternative%20Fuel%20Fact%20Brief-%20Natural%20Gas.pdf

13 "Shell Weighs Natural Gas-to-Diesel Processing Facility for Louisiana," *Wall Street Journal*, April 4, 2012, http://online.wsj.com/article/SB10001424052702304072004577323770856080102.html

14 "GTL Approaching End Of Its Road," *World Gas Intelligence*. February 18, 2009. http://www.energyintel.com/DocumentDetail.asp?Try=Yes&document_id=251811&publication_id=10

15 MIT, *The Future of Natural Gas*, 125. http://web.mit.edu/mitei/research/studies/documents/natural-gas-2011/NaturalGas_Chapter5_Demand.pdf

16 Ibid.

17 Kenneth Medlock, Amy Jaffe and Peter Hartley, *Shale Gas and U.S. National Security*, Baker Institute Energy Forum, July 2011, www.bakerinstitute.org/publications/EF-pub-DOEShaleGas-07192011.pdf

18 Based on $3.26 /gallon factory price ($2.85 cost of crude oil plus $0.41 refining cost.)

19 Vikram Rao, *Shale Gas: The Promise and the Peril*, (Research Triangle Institute Press, 2012).

20 "DOE says test shows potential for natgas hydrates," *Reuters*, May 2, 2012, http://www.reuters.com/article/2012/05/02/us-usa-natgas-hydrates-idUSBRE84119120120502

21 "The 5% Solution: Methanol Production Feedstock Diversity", Methanol Institute factsheet

22 Roberta J. Nichols, "The Methanol Story: A Sustainable Fuel for the Future," *Journal of Scientific & Industrial Research*, Vol. 62, January-February 2003, pp 97- 105, http://www.setamericafree.org/Rnichols.pdf

23 "Japan's Mitsui Chemicals to Make Methanol from CO_2," *Reuters*, August 28, 2008

24 Testimony of Vinod Khosla, Senate Foreign Relations Committee Hearing, May 16, 2006 http://lugar.senate.gov/energy/hearings/pdf/060516/Khosla_Testimony.pdf

[25] *U.S. Billion Ton Update: Biomass Supply for a Bioenergy and Bioproducts Industry*, U.S. Department of Energy, Oak Ridge National Laboratory, August 2011.

[26] For full description of the various chemical process resulting in methanol see: George Olah, Alain Goeppert and Surya Prakash, *Beyond Oil and Gas: The Methanol Economy*, (Weinheim: Wiley 2006)

[27] For detailed information about the biomass to methanol pathways and costs see: L. Bromberg and W.K. Cheng, *Methanol as an Alternative Transportation Fuel in the U.S.: Options for Sustainable and/or Energy-Secure Transportation*, Sloan Automotive Laboratory, Massachusetts Institute of Technology, September 2010.

[28] P. Sheehy, K. Law and M.D. Jackson, *Methanol Fuel Blending Characterization and Materials Compatibility*, Final Report TIAX LLC.

[29] The World Bank Global Gas Flaring Reduction, http://go.worldbank.org/Q7E8SP9J90

[30] "In North Dakota, Flames of Wasted Natural Gas the Prairie," *New York Times*, September 26, 2011, http://www.nytimes.com/2011/09/27/business/energy-environment/in-north-dakota-wasted-natural-gas-flickers-against-the-sky.html?_r=2&hp

[31] Ibid

[32] Peter Ward and Jonathan Teague (California Energy Commission), *Fifteen Years of Fuel Methanol Distribution*, presented at the XI International Symposium on Alcohol Fuels, 1996; available from http://www.energy.ca.gov/papers/CEC-999-1996-017.PDF

[33] Methanol Fuel and Fire Safety, Environmental Protection Agency, EPA 400-F-92-010, 1994, http://www.epa.gov/otaq/consumer/08-fire.pdf

[34] G. Short, "A Methanol Maritime Spillage Scenario: What If the Exxon Valdez Had Carried methanol?" 1999 World Methanol Conference, San Diego, Nov. 29-Dec. 1, 1999.

[35] Malcolm Pirnie, *Evaluation of the Fate and Transport of Methanol in the Environment*, January 1999, http://www-erd.llnl.gov/FuelsoftheFuture/pdf_files/evaluation.pdf

[36] Nichols, p. 104.

Chapter 6

Methanol Economy's Beta Site

[1] "China: The Leader in Methanol Transportation," Methanol Institute Fact Sheet, July 2011, http://methanol.org/Methanol-Basics/Resources/China-Methanol.aspx

[2] Speech by Wang Maolin, Chairman of Chinese Association of Productivity Science Honorary Chairman of China Association of Alcohol & Ether Clean Fuels and Automobiles under China Petroleum and Chemical Industry Federation, Methanol Policy Forum, Washington DC, March 27, 2012, http://www.methanol.org/Energy/Transportation-Fuel/Wang-Maolin_03_27.aspx

[3] Genia Kostka and William Hobbs, *Embedded Interests and the Managerial Local State: The Political Economy of Methanol Fuel-Switching in China*, Frankfurt School of Finance and Management Working Papers Series, February 2011.

[4] Ibid.

[5] Greg Dolan, "China Takes Gold in Methanol Fuel," *Journal of Energy Security*, October 2008.

[6] Lecture by Peng Zhigui, former Vice Governor of Shanxi Province, before the 2012 China International Alcohol and Ether Fuels Industry Development Conference, May 22, 2012

[7] Ibid.

[8] JD Power and Associates, 2012 China Dealer Attitude Study, April 22, 2012, http://autos.jdpower.com/content/press-release/hI7DlXE/2012-china-dealer-attitude-study.htm

[9] M. Wang, H. Huo, L. Johnson and D. He, *Projection of Chinese Motor Vehicle Growth, Oil Demand and CO$_2$ Emissions through 2050*, Argonne National Laboratory, ANL/ESD/06-6 http://www.transportation.anl.gov/pdfs/TA/398.pdf

Chapter 7

The Fuel We Love to Hate

[1] Larry Kudlow, "Bernanke and Ethanol Sink Egypt," *National Review Online*, January 31, 2011

[2] Michael Pollan, "Farmer in Chief," *New York Times Magazine*, October 9, 2008, http://www.nytimes.com/2008/10/12/magazine/12policy-t.html

[3] Bruce Dale, "Biofuels: Thinking Clearly about the Issues," in Daveed Gartenstein Ross and Clifford May eds. *From Energy Crisis to Energy Security*, (Washington, DC: FDD Press, 2008), p.57.

[4] See also Hosein Shapouri, James A. Duffield, and Michael Wang, "The Energy Balance of Corn Ethanol: An Update," U.S. Department of Agriculture, Office of the Chief Economist, Office of Energy Policy and New Uses, Agricultural Economic Report No. 814, http://www.usda.gov/oce/reports/energy/aer-814.pdf

5   Peter Huber, "Thermodynamics and Money," *Forbes*, October 31, 2005, http://www.forbes.com/free_forbes/2005/1031/122.html

6   Peter Cohn, "Ethanol Credits Have A Major Beneficiary In Big Oil Firms," National Journal, February 7, 2011, http://www.nationaljournal.com/daily/ethanol-credits-have-a-major-beneficiary-in-big-oil-firms-20100702

7   John M. Urbanchuk, *Contribution of the Ethanol Industry to the Economy of the United States*, February 2011, http://ethanolrfa.org/page/-/Ethanol%20Economic%20Contribution%202010%20Final%20Revised%20010411.pdf?nocdn=1

8   Neelesh Nerurkar, *U.S. Oil Imports: Context and Considerations*, Congressional Research Service, April 1, 2011, http://www.fas.org/sgp/crs/misc/R41765.pdf

9   "As Biofuels Catch On, Next Task Is to Deal With Environmental, Economic Impact," *Wall Street Journal,* March 24, 2008.

10 Xiaodong Du and Dermot J. Hayes, *The Impact of Ethanol Production on US and Regional Gasoline Markets: An Update to 2012*, Center for Agricultural and Rural Development Iowa State University, Working Paper 12-WP 528, May 2012, http://www.card.iastate.edu/publications/dbs/pdffiles/12wp528.pdf

11 "Biofuels Crime against Humanity," *BBC News*, October 27, 2007, http://news.bbc.co.uk/2/hi/americas/7065061.stm

12 "Venezuela's Chavez Slams Bush Ethanol Plan," *Reuters*, April 10, 2007.

13 "Saudi scholar warns alcohol in bio fuel is a sin," *AlArabiya.net*, February 19, 2009, http://www.alarabiya.net/articles/2009/02/19/66803.html

14 "Crude Awakening: Saudi Oil Minister Warns Against Renewable Exuberance," *Wall Street Journal*, February 11, 2009.

15 Günther Fischer, Eva Hizsnyik, Sylvia Prieler, Mahendra Shah and Harrij van Velthuizen, *Biofuels and Food Security*, International Institute for Applied Systems Analysis (IIASA), Vienna, Austria, March 2009, http://www.iiasa.ac.at/Research/LUC/Homepage-News-Highlights/OFID_IIASAPam_38_bio.pdf

16 "OPEC President Blames Ethanol from Crude Price Rise," *Marketwatch*, July 6, 2008, http://www.marketwatch.com/story/opec-president-blames-oil-prices-on-ethanol-weak-dollar-reports

17 "Beating Up on Ethanol," *Roll Call*, May 14, 2008, http://www.rollcall.com/issues/53_137/-23620-1.html

18 "Ethanol Production Capacity Over 14 Billion Gallons," *Reuters*, November 29, 2011, http://www.reuters.com/article/2011/11/29/us-usa-ethanol-production-idUSTRE7AS27P20111129

19 "The Impact of Ethanol Use on Food Prices and Greenhouse Gas Emissions," Congressional Budget Office, April 2009.

[20] John Baffes and Tassos Haniotis, *Placing the 2006/08 Commodity Price Boom into Perspective*, Policy Research Working Paper 5371, World Bank Group, July 2010, http://www-wds.worldbank.org/external/default/WDSContentServer/IW3P/IB/2010/07/21/000158349_20100721110120/Rendered/PDF/WPS5371.pdf

[21] "McCain's Farm Flop," *Fortune Magazine*, October 26, 2006, http://money.cnn.com/magazines/fortune/fortune_archive/2006/11/13/8393132/index.htm

[22] "Giant ethanol maker among Gingrich's top campaign donors," *USA Today*, December 8, 2011, http://www.usatoday.com/news/politics/story/2011-12-06/newt-gingrich-ethanol-campaign-donor/51682042/1

[23] "US Corn Ethanol was not a good Policy – Gore," *Reuters*, November 22, 2010, http://af.reuters.com/article/energyOilNews/idAFLDE6AL0YT20101122

[24] Tim Searchinger et al, "Use of U.S. croplands for biofuels increases greenhouse gases through emissions from land-use change," *Science Magazine*, February 29, 2008, p. 1238.

[25] Robert Zubrin, "In Defense of Biofuels," *The New Atlantis*, Spring 2008, http://www.thenewatlantis.com/publications/in-defense-of-biofuels

[26] Michael Wang, The Debate on Energy and Greenhouse Gas Emissions Impacts of Fuel Ethanol, Argonne National Laboratory, August 3, 2005, http://www.transportation.anl.gov/pdfs/TA/347.pdf

[27] *An Examination of the Potential for Improving Carbon/Energy Balance of Bioethanol*, A Report to IEA Bioenergy Task Force 39, February 15, 2009

[28] "Judge Blocks a California Fuel Regulation," *The New York Times*, December 29, 2011.

[29] "Everyone Hates Ethanol," *Wall Street Journal*, March 16, 2009, http://online.wsj.com/article/SB123716798764436701.html

Chapter 8

A Platform for Competition

[1] *An America that Works: Job Creation and America's Future*, McKinsey Global Institute, June 2011, http://www.mckinsey.com/Insights/MGI/Research/Labor_Markets/An_economy_that_works_for_US_job_creation

[2] "GM seeking more U.S. ethanol fueling stations," *Reuters*, February 16, 2010, http://www.reuters.com/article/2010/02/16/gm-ethanol-idUSN1619509020100216

[3] L. Bromberg and W.K. Cheng, *Methanol as an alternative transportation fuel in the US: Options for sustainable and/or energy-secure transportation*, Prepared by the Sloan Automotive Laboratory, Massachusetts Institute of Technology, September 27, 2010, p. 62

4   "Big Trucks Returned Big Profits for Detroit," *New York Times,* November 22, 2011, http://wheels.blogs.nytimes.com/2011/11/22/big-trucks-returned-big-profits-for-detroit/

5   Jameson Wetmore, "Implementing Restraint: Automobile Safety and the U.S. Debate over Technological and Social Fixes," in Jim Conley and Arlene Tigar McLaren, *Car Troubles: Critical Studies of Automobility and Auto-Mobility*, (Burlington VT: Ashgate 2009), p. 117

6   Ibid, ibid.

7   Ibid, p. 116

8   Seat Belt Use in 2010 – Use Rates in the States and Territories National Highway Traffic Safety Administration, July 2011, http://www-nrd.nhtsa.dot.gov/Pubs/811493.pdf

9   "Big Three Talk up Flex-Fuel Cars," *Marketwatch*, March 26, 2007

10 "Flex-fuel vehicles touted," *USA Today*, May 7, 2007

11 Stacy Davis, Susan Diegel and Robert Boundy, *Transportation Energy Data Book 30th Edition*, Oak Ridge National Laboratory, June 2011, Tables 4-12 and 4-13.

12 Effects of the Alternative Motor Fuels Act CAFE Incentives Policy, Report to Congress, U.S. Department of Transportation, U.S. Department of Energy, U.S. Environmental Protection Agency, March 2002, http://www.nhtsa.gov/cars/rules/rulings/CAFE/alternativefuels/AMFAReporttoCongress.pdf

Epilogue

What Would Hayek Do?

1   M.A. Adelman, "The Real Oil Problem," *Regulation* (CATO), Spring 2004

2   Friedrich Hayek, *The Road to Serfdom: Text and Documents - The Definitive Edition (The Collected Works of F.A. Hayek, Volume 2)*, (Chicago: University of Chicago Press 2007), p. 127

3   Friedrich Hayek, The Road to Serfdom: Address before the Economic Club of Detroit, April 23, 1945, typescript Hoover Institution.

4   BP Statistical Review of World Energy, June 2012, p. 6, http://www.bp.com/liveassets/bp_internet/globalbp/globalbp_uk_english/reports_and_publications/statistical_energy_review_2011/STAGING/local_assets/pdf/oil_section_2012.pdf

5   "U.S. Might Have More Oil Resources Than Saudi Arabia, But...," *Forbes*, March 29, 2012, http://www.forbes.com/sites/energysource/2012/03/29/u-s-might-have-more-oil-resources-than-saudi-arabia-but/

6   Hayek, *The Road to Serfdom*, p.71

7   Ludwig von Mises, *Human Action: A Treatise on Economics,* (Laissez Faire Books, 2008), p. 279

8   Milton Friedman, *Capitalism and Freedom*, (Chicago: University Of Chicago Press; 1 edition, 2002), p. 27

9   Ibid.

Made in the USA
Lexington, KY
06 May 2014